Allies for Enterprise

Highlights of the 1987-88
National Conferences
on Higher Education
and Economic Development

WITHDRAWN

American Association of State Colleges
and Universities

The following individuals contributed to the coordination and execution of this project:

Ralph Alterowitz
Tom Chmura
Robert Duke
Joanne Erickson
Mary Gordon
Karen Henderson
Evelyn Hively
Trudy James
Nilda Rendino
Stephanie Rendino
Helen Roberts
Carter Rowland
Allan Watson
Hal Williams

Published by American Association of State Colleges and Universities
One Dupont Circle/Suite 700
Washington, DC 20036-1192

Distributed by arrangement with
University Publishing Associates, Inc.
4720 Boston Way, Lanham, MD 20706
3 Henrietta Street, London WC2E 8LU England

Library of Congress Cataloging-in-Publication Data
    Allies for enterprise.
    p. cm.
    ISBN 0-88044-097-X. ISBN 0-88044-096-1 (pbk.)
    1. Industry and education—United States—Congresses. 2. Economic development projects—United States—Congresses. 3. Technological innovations—United States—Congresses. 4. Economic development—Effect of education on—Congresses. I. American Association of State Colleges and Universities

LC 1085.2.H55   1988   88-16976
378.103 dc19

Contents

Foreword

The Economic Development Administration (EDA) has long recognized that colleges and universities can play an important role in local economic development. For over twenty years it has administered a University Center Program, which provides seed money to help colleges and universities initiate and implement programs that address local economic development problems and needs.

In FY 1985 EDA awarded a grant to the American Association of State Colleges and Universities (AASCU) to conduct the 1986 National Conference of Higher Education and Economic Development. The success of that conference prompted EDA to provide additional financial assistance to AASCU for a series of regional conferences that would provide a forum for leaders from higher education, government, and the private sector to exchange ideas and to begin developing strategies for addressing common economic problems.

This publication contains the proceedings from those four regional conferences. Among the topics discussed at the conferences were human resource development, technology transfer, business development, international trade, and rural and urban economic development.

Whether your institution is just beginning to address economic development issues or is interested in expanding its activities in economic development, EDA hopes this report will suggest programs and approaches that are appropriate for your situation.

Orson G. Swindle, III
Assistant Secretary
for Economic Development

Preface

The American Association of State Colleges and Universities, the Stanford Research Institute, and the National Association of Management and Technical Assistance Centers, aided by a grant from the U.S. Economic Development Administration (EDA), worked in concert to develop a series of regional seminars/workshops on bridging the gap between higher education and the economic development community. Generally, the array and intensity of the discussions, which took place at conferences during 1987-88, validated the assumption that much has been done in cementing these relationships.

State agencies, universities, and businesses have been shown to complement one another, as evidenced by the numerous institutes and centers in all areas of the country. Funding sources have been varied, but EDA support has been critical to the evolution of many of these programs. While federal funds have served as catalysts to initiate resource centers, states that have an enlightened view of support for AASCU institutions in these endeavors have achieved high levels of success. Frank Newman's book, *Choosing Quality: Reducing Conflict Between the State and the University* (Education Commission of the States, 1987) delineates how such support enhances the growth of the university.

The AASCU institutions, using entrepreneurial approaches and seeking support from private and public agencies, have responded dramatically to the needs of their constituents. Urban universities have tended to emphasize technology transfer, incubators, and business development, while rural universities tend to work principally with agricultural/business issues and small business enterprises.

More recently, however, with resources becoming more limited, AASCU institutions find themselves forced to compensate for lack of outreach from land-grant universities. This leads to neglect of the rural constituencies, which are often considered less glamorous or attractive by public and private funding agencies. Unfortunately, one notion that surfaced in the workshop/

seminar discussions was the necessity to heed the needs of the rural populations, particularly as the numbers of the aging increase and as support from university centers shifts to urban environments. Many AASCU institutions have recognized this need and have redefined missions in that context.

As competition for available resources becomes more fierce, AASCU institutions will be forced to make choices but, hopefully, state budgets will be increased to support AASCU programs that serve a vital need.

The partnership between academe and economic development ventures, at times, leads to some tension as entrepreneurs, hoping for monetary gain, sometimes forget the central mission of the university. Serving students and teaching may become secondary to efforts at catering to narrow self-interest. On the other hand, students in some institutions play a vital role in this partnership, helping in both research and technical transfer. Often, particularly in rural areas, undergraduate and graduate students aid constituents with budgets, cost effectiveness in product development, and communication enhancement.

Despite the minor nuisances that might arise in working out partnerships, AASCU institutions have taken a leading role in making these liaisons work. The seminars have stimulated many of the participants to seek additional ways to heighten efforts to strive for quality in these relationships.

J. Carter Rowland
Consultant, AASCU
May 1988

Introduction

In 1987, the American Association of State Colleges and Universities (AASCU) received a grant from the U.S. Department of Commerce Economic Development Administration (EDA) to conceive, plan, and coordinate a series of regional conferences. The series was to follow up activities to the 1986 National Conference on Higher Education and Economic Development, which had also stemmed from an EDA grant to AASCU. These activities arose from the association's ongoing commitment to supporting the efforts of public colleges and universities to improve the quality of life in their communities.

The four regional conferences represented in this book were held during 1987-88 and sponsored by AASCU, SRI International, the National Association of Management and Technical Assistance Centers, and EDA. The conferences served as forums for addressing the role of public colleges and universities in fostering economic development in their communities, regions, states, and the nation. The extreme importance of and widespread interest in this topic were reflected in the diversity of conference participants: college and university presidents, faculty members, corporate heads, association heads, and civic leaders.

This book presents four summaries written for AASCU by SRI International, as part of the EDA-funded activity, of the economic challenges now being faced by the major regions of the nation. Each regional summary is followed by the program agenda for that regional conference, in turn followed by excerpts from several speeches given at that conference.

It is the hope of all at AASCU that readers will find this publication an indispensable resource for establishing or improving programs at their institutions or in their communities, for discovering what other institutions and communities are doing, and for learning more about the interdependence of public colleges and universities and the local/regional economy. Such endeavors will benefit not only all of public higher education but also the nation's economy and—ultimately—its quality of life.

Editor's Note

During the course of the four regional conferences in 1987-88, over sixty speeches, workshops, and panel discussions took place. For practical reasons, they could not be printed in their entirety in one volume, nor would it be advisable to do so. First, the actual verbatim proceedings would fill two or three volumes, and the unedited speeches—with all the faults and foibles that usually characterize informal talk—would make laborious reading. Second, conference room arrangements and equipment limitations prevented the tape recording of some presentations.

Among those speeches that were tape recorded, some could not be transcribed because of inaudibility, probably resulting from poor room acoustics. Hence, the excerpts appearing in this book are from speeches that were clearly audible on the tape or for which the speaker provided AASCU with hard copy of the text by March 1988.

In selecting the excerpts, I first eliminated all passages that were too vaguely audible on the tape, ambiguous in meaning, conversational in nature, extremely general in content, rambling, or duplicative or previous speeches. From the remaining passages I attempted to distill those of greatest potential interest and use to the reader. Thus, most of the excerpts chosen contain detailed information about a specific institution or region, real-life examples of programs, and/or helpful advice.

The selected excerpts were then edited lightly for clarity and conciseness, with as much care as possible taken to avoid changing the speakers' intended meanings and to match the right passages with the right voices on the tape. If I have inadvertently changed any messages or mismatched speakers to speeches, I apologize.

Despite the limitations inherent in any effort to publish a large amount of tape-recorded material, any reader concerned about higher education's role in economic development should find this publication of considerable value.

Higher Education, Economic Development, and the Midwest

Overview

The United States has entered a new era of global competition and falling world commodity prices. The midwestern region of the United States has been hard hit because of its traditional reliance on a diminishing agricultural industry and major manufacturing industries—primarily auto making, which is vulnerable to increasing foreign competition.

The traditional competitive advantages enjoyed by the region—including abundant natural resources, a large industrial labor force, technological leadership, and a critical mass of traditional buyers and suppliers in the region—have in many cases been counterbalanced by other nations.

To achieve a competitive advantage and build a dynamic economy, the midwestern region needs to adopt new economic development approaches. Some key industries and firms are, in fact, making vital, positive changes. In manufacturing, changes include flexible specialization replacing mass production, greater efficiency in mass production, and greater emphasis on value-added products. In agriculture as well, changes include product specialization emphasizing value-added products rather than mass production technology. A successful economic transition will be based on improved access to advanced technology, a skilled and adaptable work force, and access to risk capital.

State agencies, educational institutions, and industries in the region all face a new set of economic challenges:

Human resource development. The region must have a skilled and adaptable work force, from top managers to first-line technicians. Developing this work force requires new flexible education and training approaches, from community colleges to flagship universities.

Advanced technology development. Advanced technology produces the foundation for future economic development. Universities are a major source of advanced technology and have a long-term commitment to basic and applied research. Academic institutions and private businesses in the Midwest, however, need to develop more effective mechanisms to bring technology to the market place.

• *Technology transfer.* A major problem facing the Midwest is effective use of existing technology. The region needs to develop more effective mechanisms to channel university-generated research to private industry and facilitate industry use of new technology through technical assistance.

• *Business development.* New businesses can be stimulated through a number of mechanisms. Universities can help foster business development by developing innovative intellectual-property policies, business incubators, technology parks, and direct support to business in technology application, international marketing, and management education.

Some colleges and universities in the region are making a special effort to help industry adapt and to prepare their students for new economic realities. Other institutions want to do more, but haven't developed the capacity as yet. The midwestern regional seminar reviewed these efforts and explored what more could be done to help the region.

The Historical Role of Midwestern Higher Education

Midwestern colleges and universities have traditionally been linked to the region's economic base. This tradition includes land-grant, research, technical, state, and community colleges. Until World War II, some of the region's key institutions built their reputations as sources of agricultural education and research. The Morrill Act of 1862 established land-grant colleges in each state to act as agriculture, natural resource, and mechanical arts centers. They were closely tied to virtually every sector of the U.S. economy, providing a broad spectrum of services including the provision of skilled graduates on the one end and contractual problem-specific research and technical consulting on the other.

After World War II, the federal government made its first major peace-time investment in basic research. As a result, many universities began to diversify and strengthen their basic research capabilities. In addition, many new graduate research universities sprouted in the 1950s and 1960s and drew support from several public and private agencies and industry. The subjects of research and education became less dependent on the nation's technological and economic position in world competition. Also, national needs for specific research were minimal during these early postwar years. When Europe and Japan recovered from their postwar economic and social wounds and reentered international competition, the United States was not prepared to meet the onslaught of aggressive competition. Universities and colleges have accordingly been slow to adjust to the realities of increased global competition, but many are taking steps today to reestablish and strengthen their linkages with the private sector, to better facilitate economic growth.

The Midwest today has superior educational resources and produces top-quality science and engineering faculty and graduates. The Midwest ranks in the top one-third in the quality of its science and engineering faculty, in the number of science and engineering graduates per capita, in expenditures per pupil, in college test scores, and in the percentage of students attending two-year colleges. In recent years, midwestern states have increased overall levels of support for university programs and students. Most midwestern states have established state programs to foster linkages between industry and university R&D.

The problem for the Midwest is not the lack of a strong educational base, but rather underutilization of these resources by industry, government, and the institutions themselves. The intellectual capacity generated by these institutions has not yet been adequately tapped and channeled to enhance the region's economic development.

Midwestern Higher Education's Responses to Industry Changes

Because of the rapidly changing demands of the new global economy, colleges and universities in the Midwest will need to play a more aggressive role in the region's economic development. Some of the most critical challenges facing the Midwest, and higher education in particular, were discussed in the midwestern regional seminar: human resources development, advanced technology development, technology transfer, and business development. Many of the region's colleges and universities have begun to respond to the changing demands of the postindustrial economy by strengthening their capacity in each—or, in some cases, all—of the four topics. The institutions and programs listed below have been chosen as examples of initiatives that higher education can take to help enhance the region's competitiveness.

Human Resources Development

To adapt to changes in the new global economy—which include increasing challenges of foreign competition, the impact of changing technologies and consumer demands, and new corporate structures—the midwestern states must cultivate a skilled and adaptable work force. Skills at all levels, from shop floor assemblers and technicians to top-level engineers and managers, must be enhanced. This process requires major increases in both private and public investments in training and retraining of workers. For universities and community colleges, as well as state-sponsored and other technical centers, it means a stronger commitment to developing or expanding existing science, engineering, and business management education, including extension programs for professionals. Institutions need to distinguish between long-term and short-term educational needs and provide for them by building on their historical capacity. Research universities can train Ph.D.s who provide basic research for long-term application; state universities can provide for mid- and short-term needs through four-year and two-year degree programs and applied research; community colleges and private technical institutions can provide fundamental vocational training for immediate industry application.

University of Wisconsin, Stout. Stout is one of thirteen publicly funded centers in Wisconsin offering industrial, vocational, and home economics education. It consists of undergraduate and graduate programs in industrial science, technology, home economics, applied arts, and others. The programs are career oriented, and designed to meet state and national needs in each of these areas. For example, Stout is known as a major center for training technicians for the packaging industry. Stout has a well-developed board of business advisers who actively participate in university planning and development.

Sinclair Community College (OH). The college cosponsors (with GMF Robotics) a Robotics Training Center, a training site for southern Ohio residents and for GMF Robotics vendors and suppliers. It supplies customized training in basic skills as well as engineering and management courses and serves as a leading example of new human resource development programs.

Advanced-Technology Development

Improved access to advanced-technology development is central to enhanced economic competitiveness of the midwestern region. The adaptability of its key industries—ranging from agriculture to auto manufacturing—will increasingly depend on advances in new technologies, particularly in automated manufacturing, advanced materials, information systems, and biotechnology. Colleges and universities play a salient role in research on and development of driving technologies by providing a continuum of advanced-technology activities ranging from long-term basic research to short-term applied research with immediate industrial application. Most research conducted at universities is basic, although some of the basic research eventually gives rise to new start-ups. In fulfilling their economic role within the region, midwestern institutions need to recognize and build on their historical research capacity. Research universities, land-grant schools, technology schools, state universities, and community colleges each offer different capabilities. Yet each can contribute distinctive strengths to the overall economic competitiveness of the region and nation.

Basic research:

Purdue University Computer-Integrated Design and Manufacturing and Automation Center (CIDMAC). Funded largely by private member companies, CIDMAC conducts basic research in the following areas: computer-aided design (CAD), computer-aided manufacturing (CAM), machine vision, and robotics. Research is intended to decrease the cost of low-volume manufacturing of products by increasing the efficiency of the manufacturing process. With NSF funding, CIDMAC established in 1985 an Engineering Research Center for Intelligent Manufacturing Systems. The overall objective of the center is to create flexible product factories (factories of the future) and to develop a methodology for planning and operating the factories. Seven corporations participate in the ERC as "partners," each paying $200,000 per year for five years for access to university labs and advanced techniques. In addition, ten affiliate companies are involved in the program, each contributing $25,000 per year for the opportunity to attend meetings and receive reports of research results.

University of Michigan. The University of Michigan has recently established a multidisciplinary initiative in advanced automated manufacturing. The university operates two large research centers—the Center for Research in Integrated Manufacturing (CRIM) and the Center for Machine Intelligence (CMI). With an annual budget of more than $9 million, CRIM draws together nearly 100 professors from five departments, primarily electrical engineering and computer science. Research focuses on robotics, particularly software design, programming, and machine vision. CMI consists of eighteen engineering faculty and has an annual budget of more than $2.87 million. Research projects focus on machine vision, robotics, artificial intelligence, and computer architecture.

Applied Research
Cleveland Advanced Manufacturing Program (CAMP). One of the six Edison Technology Centers, CAMP was established to stimulate the development and application of new computer-based manufacturing technologies that can benefit northern Ohio industries. With initial funding from the Edison Program and matching funds from the private sector, CAMP offers research, training, and technology transfer for its clients. Three academic participants in CAMP are Case Western Reserve

7

University, Cleveland State University, and Cuyahoga Community College. CAMP's research projects are contractually performed for business on a proprietary basis. Case Western offers basic and applied research focused on automation and intelligent systems. Cleveland State, through the Advanced Manufacturing Center of its Fenn College of Engineering, offers companies applied research in computer-aided design and manufacturing and in sensor applications. Cuyahoga Community College is completing a Unified Technologies Center, which will custom-train industrial workers to use technologically advanced systems.

Michigan Biotechnology Institute (MBI). MBI is a nonprofit corporation organized by the Governor's Task Force on High Technology. The corporation serves as a link between universities and industry in fostering commercialization of biotechnology products and processes, and in conducting problem-focused research and technology transfer to industry. It focuses on applied R&D of renewable resource-based biotechnology. Project areas include: (1) fermentation and biomaterials products technology, (2) industrial enzyme technology, and (3) waste treatment biotechnology. Some examples of research performed at MBI are the development of new enzymes for the production of sweetening agents from corn starch and the production of improved waste treatment processes that provide by-product gas energy from industrial and municipal wastes. Many of the research projects take place at or in conjunction with Michigan universities, particularly Michigan State University.

University of Illinois, Urbana-Champaign Biotechnology Research Center and Plant and Animal Science Research Center. The Biotechnology Research Center is an interdisciplinary program designed to promote collaborative biotechnology-related research projects with faculty in the college of agriculture, medicine, and veterinarian medicine, and the schools of chemical sciences and life sciences. The center, through an Industrial Affiliates Program, will also foster university-industry joint research and faculty consulting in bioprocess engineering and other areas. Research will focus on such areas as recombinant DNA technology, image analysis, and protein engineering. The

Plant and Animal Research Center will provide R&D initiatives and education programs focusing on corn and soybean germplasm development for higher-value-added products.

Technology Transfer
Although the Midwest has solid academic research capacity and trains the top third of the nation's graduates, its problem is channeling technology to industry users. State universities can—and are beginning to—address the historically difficult problem of moving technology from the university to the region's economy. To do so, the universities, often working with state programs, are developing programs that provide such services as networking with businesses and industry, information and finance brokering, and various forms of technical assistance:

Michigan's Technology Deployment Service (TDS). TDS is a state-sponsored program designed to assist small and medium-size firms in adopting advanced computer-based manufacturing tools and methods. Industry support services include: (1) technical assistance in designing a customized training program to support use of new technology, (2) grant procurement for training programs, and (3) consulting on new manufacturing technologies. TDS Training Associates consists of faculty members of Michigan community colleges and private consulting and industry specialists.

Ohio University Innovation Center. The center was established in 1982 to encourage growth of technology-oriented business. Services offered to industry by the center include access to university engineers and scientists for consultation and research assistance; technical training for personnel; identification of product markets; management, finance, and marketing assistance; quality control and quality assurance testing; computer services; and other activities.

Ohio Technology Transfer Organization (OTTO). OTTO was developed by the Ohio Board of Regents in 1982 to provide coordinated access to technology information and technical services available through Ohio educational institutions. A network of agents located at twenty-eight colleges and universities statewide links information and experts to the Ohio businesses that need help. Programs include the Ohio Industrial Training Program (OIDP) and linked start-up training programs for entrepreneurial management and engineering skills.

Business Development

New economic factors are prompting both the dissolution and creation of many companies in the region. The stimulation of new businesses is vitally important to the region's economy. Colleges, universities, and technology centers are recognizing their potential for providing the technological, managerial, or financial assistance needed for businesses and industries to meet competitive challenges. Institutions can offer a continuum of resources, including directly promoting new-business formation, by amending intellectual property and promotional policies, creating new business incubators that link new firms with university resources, and creating industrial parks that allow university land to be used to form centers for business development.

University of Illinois, Chicago Technology Park. The Chicago Technology Park was established in 1982 by the State of Illinois and City of Chicago. The park is operated by a nonprofit corporation and focuses primarily on biotechnology businesses. Services provided include consulting with university faculty, computer and library facilities, and contacts with venture capital sources, in addition to provision of laboratory and office facilities.

Illinois Community College Business Center Program. All thirty-nine community college districts in Illinois operate Business Centers. The program is state funded, with a budget of $3.7 million. (The median school budget is $75,000.) Each center offers economic development activities tailored to the local community. Activities fall into three general categories: customized job training, entrepreneurship training, and commercialization and industrial development assistance. Some centers also run labor management councils, while others serve as business incubators and contract procurement brokers.

Oakland University, Oakland Technology Park (MI). Currently well into its early stages of development, OTP is planned to encompass about 1,200 acres in Oakland County, Michigan. This high-technology park is designed for research, development, high-technology operations (such as data processing and communications), design, and engineering. Companies that have built facilities in OTP include Camerica, GMF Robotics, World Computer, and Schostak's. It is projected that about 52,000 new jobs will be created in the primary impact area of the park by 1995. OTP is to serve as a link between the business community and Oakland University for education and joint research ventures.

Michigan State University, Neogen. In 1981 Michigan State University and the State of Michigan helped finance the creation of Neogen Biological Corporation. Neogen is a for-profit biotechnology R&D company. As an off-campus site, Neogen provides entrepreneurial opportunities for the university's faculty researchers and facilitates university-industry research collaboration.

Challenges for Midwestern Higher Education

The Midwest has a unique resource base that will help the region adapt to the rapidly changing economy. The key challenge is now for institutions of higher education to focus and apply their resources in ways that will enhance overall economic development in each state. In the future, academic institutions will need to address systematically the issues of human resources development, advanced technology development, technology transfer, and business development so that they can have the broadest possible impact on the economy. In expanding their role, universities and colleges must distinguish where their long-term and near-term strengths are and how these strengths can be applied so as to best contribute to the Midwest's economic growth. Some critical challenges facing colleges and universities are summarized as follows:

Human resources. Universities and colleges must make a commitment to long-term institutional changes by enhancing support of interdisciplinary engineering and technology education programs. This must be done in addition to expanding or strengthening four-year and two-year technical programs that supply such a large part of today's labor force.

Advanced-technology development. Schools need to discover their strengths, rather than emulate others, and concentrate on reallocating resources to basic technology strengths, particularly interdisciplinary research programs. In the near term, universities and colleges need to strengthen their applied-technology capacity to better focus on areas relevant to multiple segments of the region's economy. Institutions must also understand the distinction between applied and direct, hands-on utilization of science and technology and build more effective ongoing linkages to industry.

Technology transfer. The challenge is to create a range of effective university-business linkages responsive to the dynamics of the private market place. Universities and colleges need to modify their "culture" to offer incentives for faculty members to provide technical assistance to businesses in the region.

Business development. Colleges and universities need to take more of a leadership position in stimulating the development and expansion of businesses by changing their policies not only to tolerate but support the translation of intellectual capital into new enterprise, and by helping to sustain such enterprise through its early stages of development.

There are a number of obstacles to each type of university-industry relationship that need to be addressed. First, the cultural barrier between the faculty and the business community is difficult to overcome. This attitudinal problem is based partly on a mutual lack of understanding as well as a lack of incentives for either side. Many educators may see economic development as irrelevant, or even contradictory, to the university's mission. Businesses may not be aware of university resources, or may fear that faculty, asserting their right to academic freedom, will not perform research that is applicable enough to specific company or industry needs.

Second, the organizational structure of institutions can pose a serious barrier, both for faculty and private business representatives. Barriers include cumbersome policies eatablished by many institutions that discourage faculty from forming cooperative relationships with business, industry, and government. Proposed research efforts with universities often require complex administrative processing, with the final agreement often modified to suit the institution far more than the individual researcher or the client. Some colleges and universities in the region are modifying their organizational structure to better foster university-industry interaction. One example is the establishment of industrial advisory boards.

Third, the absence of mechanisms for interdisciplinary research makes innovative research, training, or education quite difficult. However, as advanced sciences and technologies become increasingly multidisciplinary, many institutions are making changes, such as creating independent research centers and institutes or amending research application procedures, to accommodate and promote new private-sector research.

Agenda

Midwestern Regional Seminar
April 23-24, 1987
Chicago, Illinois

Tour of Chicago Technology Park

Welcoming Remarks: George Ayers, President, Chicago State University (IL)

Panel Discussion: Perspectives on the Economy of the Midwest and the Role of Higher Education in Future Economic Development
Moderator: Charles Bartsch, Director, Economic Development Group, Northeast/Midwest Institute
Presenters: William Hogan, Vice President for Corporate Affairs, Honeywell, Inc.; Robert Swanson, President, University of Wisconsin-Stout; Jamie Kenworthy, Manager, Science and Technology Programs, Michigan Strategic Fund

Seminar Overview: The Higher Education-Economic Development Connection
Introduction: Hal Williams, Executive Secretary, National Association of Management and Technical Assistance Centers; Helen Roberts, Director, Office of Community Development and Public Service, AASCU
Presenter: James Gollub, Senior Policy Analyst, Center for Economic Competitiveness, SRI International

Panel Discussion: College and University Initiatives to Address Economic Issues in the Midwest
Moderator: Margaret Wireman, Director, Wisconsin Small Business Development Center

•*Technology Transfer*: John Entorf, Associate Dean, School of Industry and Technology, University of Wisconsin-Stout; Larry Schneider, Project Director for Cooperative Manufacturing Technology, Case International Harvester

•*Advanced Technology Development:* Donald Langenberg, Chancellor, University of Illinois at Chicago; Anthony Ponter, Dean of Engineering, Cleveland State University (OH)

•*New Business Support:* Lynn Berger, Assistant Director, Illinois Community College Board

•*Farm Debt and the Agricultural Crisis*: Donald Holt, Director, Illinois Agricultural Experiment Station

Luncheon Address: Mary Clutter, Senior Science Advisor, National Science Foundation

Luncheon Roundtable Discussions

Concurrent Workshops: Human Resources and Economic Shifts, Technology Transfer, Advanced Technology Development, New Business Support, Farm Debt and the Agricultural Crisis Workshop Reports Closing Remarks: Steven Gage, President, Midwest Technology Development Institute

Closing Remarks: Steven Gage, President, Midwest Technology Development Institute

Excerpts

Charles Bartsch

...Somewhat good news is that the economy of the Midwest began in 1987 in the best condition of the decade. The region's population has generally stabilized. Unemployment is still higher than the national average in many states, but it has dropped. There are new jobs being created, new businesses being born, and the states themselves in the Midwest are generally in healthy fiscal condition. Continued low interest rates and continued low rates of inflation have helped fuel a boom in consumer borrowing and spending that has helped the Midwest. This has been reflected in èmployment growth in the region's service sector as well as in finance and retail trade. These positive indicators have a soft underbelly, though: there are other economic factors that have fostered a sense of uncertainty about the future. These include record federal deficits and the spiraling trade deficit.

But a real cause for concern in the Midwest is the fact that the overall economic base of the nation is undergoing a significant transformation, and the downturn in traditional American industries that began with the recession in 1980 has become a real economic shake-out. The Midwest, which has long been reliant on heavy manufacturing, has borne the brunt of these changes: in technology, in available employment opportunities, in skills requirements, and in business management practices. Between 1979 and 1984 the six states of the industrial Midwest lost one million manufacturing jobs—60 percent of the national total manufacturing jobs lost. Moreover, many of these so-called dislocated workers remain unemployed. In September 1986, 20 percent of all workers dislocated since 1980 lived in just three states: Illinois, Michigan, and Ohio. In human terms, this 20 percent translates into 183,000 people; that is a lot of disrupted households, a lot of reduced economic activity, and a lot of reliance on public support services....

Other economic issues facing the Midwest include how to restore productivity. There are ways of introducing new technologies into existing industry, and these must be pursued. CAD/CAM and such activity needs to be explored, and its full applications introduced. There is going to be some need for corporate restructuring to make it more flexible and responsive. *Business Week* has said that competitiveness is going to be replaced as a buzzword by corporate flexibility. We are going to need efforts toward worker literacy and retraining including what *Business Week* again calls "getting man and machine to live happily together ever after." We're going to need to invest in research and development and educational programs and facilities....

Another issue the Midwest needs to address is how to promote entrepreneurship and new business formation. There's a need for a whole new crop of public-private partnerships, funding, facilities management, and development in technical support. This is a great opportunity for education to get involved, and education institutions have begun to do this well. We need better public-sector capacity to assist development....

Another issue facing the Midwest is how to help the aging industrial communities with severely depressed economies that have been unable to amass the necessary investment capital and manpower resources to reverse their decline. There are still considerable pockets of deep depression in the Midwest, and until these areas are given some opportunity and helped to recover in some way, the regional economy as a whole will continue to be a little wobbly....

We also need to find out and address how to reverse the economic decline in the midwestern farm belt. Some of the best news is that midwestern state and local public and private officials have recruited creative thinkers and are beginning to structure highly innovative and flexible programs to deal with the issues. They are helping to generate new businesses, revive viable older ones, create new quality jobs, and uncover new capital sources....

Universities are becoming larger players in state and local development strategies and activities, and they should be. They have considerable and diverse resources that can offer great benefits for community and human resource development, and these resources are taking on an increasing importance in an era of federal budget cuts and fiscal restraint....The most successful efforts are based on frank dialogue between state government officials, university officials, and private business owners and managers. And these efforts have the best effect when they link the academic facility and research strength of the university with the economic labor force and the quality-of-life advantages of their communities....

William Hogan

..The "outstate" areas, which have depended on agriculture, taconite, and steel industries, and the "instate" areas, which have the more high-tech industries—3M, Honeywell, Control Data, Cray Research, and so forth—are two completely different kinds of economies, but two economies that now find themselves struggling, in my opinion, as they go toward the next century, because they've got to find ways to transfer technology to "outstate" areas and economically develop them.

The state, as a whole, is doing well....We have a governor who is promoting education, and senators and representatives alike doing the same. We have an "instate/outstate situation in which the outstate jobs have diminished and revenues have diminished as a result of agriculture and steel industry. But we have a fairly healthy state and a strong populace. We have, within the Twin Cities area, something called the high-tech corridor development, which is a parcel of land set aside or partitioned to attract new industries to the Twin Cities. (If you would like to start a new company, we'll be glad to assign land to you for a certain price and support you and set you up in the Twin Cities!) We are also trying to develop applied research centers in the outstate areas and would encourage that kind of development. All of this is linked heavily to the University of Minnesota, which has 10-12 special institutes and applied research centers. I'll just name a few: Mineral Resource/Research Center, the Biological Process Technology Institute, Micro Electronics Information Science Institute....

The University of Minnesota has a supercomputer institute, as do the five NSF centers in the United States: San Diego, Princeton, the Norman center, Carnegie Mellon, Illinois, and Cornell. At the supercomputer institute we're trying to take the technology in supercomputers and somehow apply that to our companies in the Minnesota area or anywhere. For those of you in industry, you know it's difficult to use or get our colleagues involved in the use of supercomputers in production-line matters at this point in time. It is difficult to sell a supercomputer to an industry to chase or pursue current business because supercomputers are things that you need for businesses at least 5-10 years out. So, to invest in that kind of research takes a long vision on the part of the company....

We need a lot of help in interpreting service industries to companies....The first problem is how universities can take supercomputers and use them as service functions to provide service to companies, get the companies into the business, get them moving their businesses to be more competitive, and then send those same companies away from them and move them up. That's one thing we need badly, and something many of our companies are struggling with today....

I'm convinced that to be competitive, we're going to have to find better ways to put high tech into our business. Let me give you an example: manufacturing automation. There has got to be a reason why there are fifty-nine supercomputers located in Japan today, being used for real-time computation of factory configuration and delivering a product. If one can take the delivery of product from concept all the way to model and shorten that by one year, six months, then one will have shortened the entire production cycle and one may become much more competitive, with competitors here or elsewhere....

Robert Swanson

...The dairy industry has suffered from many of the same economic setbacks as have other areas of agriculture. Prices have fallen and, at the same time, improved technology of various kinds has resulted in fewer farms being able to produce much larger quantities of milk. The result has been a need to broaden the economic base of the district in which we live....

Sufficient resources exist to make the Third Congressional District a much stronger force in the economy of the state. What is needed is some sort of centralized leadership to determine direction and challenge to get this district moving with a new momentum....

Universities—not particularly Stout, because our mission has kept us involved in economic development for a long time—but most universities have been rather wary about getting involved in economic development....But our colleges and universities have always been economic development agencies. If you look at our traditional roles of research, public service, and instruction, those things have always resulted in economic development. The change is that now we are directly focusing on and claiming that we are doing things for economic development, and that is making a difference....

As we looked at the five members of the UW system, the five universities in that area, we found that we at Stout were strong in tourism and manufacturing. UW River Falls is outstanding in agriculture. Platteville has engineering, Eau Claire has business, and La Crosse has programs in recreation and health. We found that we were not in competition with each other, and that operating as a group, we covered all phases of economic development possibilities in western Wisconsin....

Jamie Kenworthy

The question that started to haunt me is, "If you were sitting here in 1950 in a conference of people from the Midwest, and you knew what was coming in terms of the world economy playing a much larger role, in the domestic and international competitive threat, what solutions would you recommend?" Two of the classic solutions you would recommend for the Midwest would be to spend a lot on higher education, and to encourage your corporations to spend a lot on R&D. Those would be two logical strategies to meet a long-term economic development threat. The problem, and why the question haunts me, is that that's what we've done for the last thirty years. As a region, we've spent much more on higher education than have other regions. I often greet the graduates of our institutions on the coast, and we have our corporations. Michigan, for instance, has been No. 2 or 3 in industrial R&D....

The issue we have to start addressing is not so much what resources we need, but *how* those resources are being spent. Because even if we can convince governors to spend more on higher education or do all these programs, that's only going to essentially add to the current cost of doing business in the region. We have to start looking at the *behavioral* issues, or else we'll be fighting for larger and larger percentages of smaller and smaller pies....

We have seen a policy of federal disinvestment in our R&D higher education structure in this country. There has been a shift from civilian to military R&D: 50/50 in the 1980s, 72/38 today. Capital expenditures for higher education and science and engineering instruction have also shifted: $207 million in 1976, $143 million uncorrected dollars in 1984—a cut of from 20-12 percent in the overall budgets.

If you look at what corporations used to spend for university contract research, 1-2 percent of the university's budget used to come from private corporations. It is now up to 5 or 6 percent. That shows a growing marriage of the two institutions sort of fumbling toward each other, but one of the reasons that increase is there, is that the federal government has lowered the base, upon which the corporations are looking better and better. The federal government is now spending $50 billion on R&D. If you add up all the state programs we're doing right now (I'm not talking about support for higher education, but all the tech-transfer programs, all the centers of excellence, all the things we have), that's about $500 million. That gives you some sense of scale of how locally we're taxing ourselves to try to address these innovation needs and what the federal government has been doing....

We've learned in the last ten or twenty years that there's no natural process of innovation: there's no natural process by which basic research gets translated into applied research, gets translated into a commercializable product. If that system worked, we wouldn't be where we are today....I'm not trying to deny the validity of the definitions of basic vs. applied research; I'm saying there hasn't been an overall strategy by the institutions that are in charge of that basic research, corporations; "applied" and "commercializable" overlap. There hasn't been an overall strategy about what problems we're seeking to address, so it hasn't been directed basic research. it hasn't been *directed* applied research. It hasn't been *directed* commercializable strategies. Until the culture of the different institutions changes, it's not going to get any better, even if we reverse those disastrous federal numbers that we all know are there in terms of disinvesting in the science base of this country. What are we doing about it? Many states are going to work with small businesses, mostly because that's the main source of jobs, and because they've discovered that when you work with small businesses, they actually listen to you, and there's some change in behavior. When you go to a large organization, it's unclear who makes decisions, and it's unclear what behavior might be changed. So it makes sense to try to work with small businesses....

When you put together the meetings of industry and government, or industries and universities and government, when you put together the consortium, if you look at what works and what doesn't work, you find the collaborations are built on *personal relationships*. They're built on personal levels of trust. It takes time to develop that. You can have a great need, but you have to essentially invest in people and personal relationships because no one trusts one another until that happens....Collaboration depends on personal relationships, on finding agents of change. It depends on setting a realistic agenda of what will be done by when and by whom and what the product is. My discovery is that I don't think universities are meant to be businesses, and they're also poor at creating strategic business plans and taking resources. But essentially, when you're performing contract research or a consortial role, you're functioning like a business. You're taking resources and promising to do certain things by a certain time. Time scales in universities and in corporations are very different. Universities generally have to learn more about how to do a strategic business plan and how to articulate what a market is....Universities think about economic development in 15–30-year time horizons...but product cycles are collapsing from 12-10-7-5 years. Mazda is able to create a car in 2–3 years, but it still takes Ford and GM five years from the start of concept to putting it out the door. So universities have to collapse their time horizons if they're going to respond....

John Entorf

The people at Case International Harvester were interested in becoming competitive and remaining competitive, and there were about three goals they wanted to accomplish with their "Cooperative Manufacturing Technology" project. They wanted to consolidate all the manufacturing at one location. In doing that, they wanted to develop a state-of-the-art manufacturing facility that would be competitive and adaptable to change. They also wanted to improve the productivity of the plant to make it competitive worldwide. The question came up, of course, if they were going to do that, they needed to select a site....There was a rather intensive company project to identify a site and identify what needed to be done. Basically, the Wisconsin facility was selected because it was reasonably new. It was built in the late or mid-1970s and was fairly clutter free....

Some goals to be achieved in this particular project: one was to consolidate all of the product lines. Another was to develop a state-of-the-art manufacturing facility utilizing both advanced technology as well as manufacturing methodology and management, all of which was available from the university....

Another reason the Wausau site was selected was that the plant had a contract, a federal military contract from Tenaco, which is the parent company of Case, and they've done an excellent job on it. They've been able to upgrade their workers, train their workers, and beat by a substantial margin the cost production of this particular unit in Newport News, Virginia. So they had a basis from which to argue. They also wanted the plant to be a flexible rather than "hard" automated plant....

Some assistance Case International has provided: the first thing to be done—a cooperative effort between Case and Stout faculty—was to develop a detailed plant layout. They were going to convert the plant to manufacture new product lines. We had to go from a single assembly facility or assembly line to multiple assembly lines. In that plant layout, they designed two detailed assembly lines for mixed boat production of two models. That activity involved both cell analysis and computer simulation. In all of this, part of the grant was utilized to acquire software and hardware to support the project. Additionally, it supports the university. They are, if you will, investing in new automation for this year. By August of this year they will have invested $17 million in new equipment....They also provide some small additions to the facility that currently are absent in terms of new building construction....

Much of the assistance provided at Wausau comes as what we call miniprojects. When we wrote the proposal to do the work over there, we knew the kinds of things that were going to be needed, but we didn't know how long they would take or exactly how they were going to be handled. We wrote in a portion of the money, and a rather substantial portion, the first year for what we call the miniproject, and after getting the project started, our manager would sit down with managers from Case and decide which kinds of projects were most important. We would then write smaller contracts for individual faculty members or groups of faculty members to address, involving such things as just-in-time delivery vendor relations, air quality analysis, marketing analysis, and so on....

This project offers some substantial benefits. A benefit to the state and the community is that Case will invest a substantial amount of money in this project—about $50 million in new technology, and a lot of equipment in Wausau right now will be replaced with equipment that exists in other plants that are being closed. A lot of facility remodeling will be done. Some new employees will be added....

Donald Langenberg

About five years ago it became clear that the economy of the State of Illinois was not in good shape, that it was not in the midst of a temporary downturn but rather in the midst of a major decline....The notion that high tech had something to do with the revitalization of the economy became popular. Both the governor of Illinois and the mayor of Chicago appointed task forces on high technology....The task forces were remarkably consistent in their recommendations....One of the things they found was that although Illinois had nearly all of the ingredients for the development of high technology, some things were missing. One was a communication network between university laboratories and Illinois industry. There was little communication with the financial sector, little understanding of how the process works, and little understanding among the news media. So, because of that, and, indeed, largely because of one of the cochairs of the mayor's task force on high technology, Walter Massey of the University of Chicago, an organization called the Chicago High Technology Association was formed. This is a not-for-profit organization committed to fostering and developing economic development in technology-based industries, both high and low and old and new, through information dissemination and transfer. If you like, you can think of it as a kind of network-generating organization. It helps people understand what is out there and how they can get to it. It has monthly programs for discussing financing and marketing and examples of successes. Participants talk about technology applications and about what's going on at the universities. The association has a quarterly magazine called The *Tech Connection* that helps spread the word. There is a membership directory so that one can, if one wants, find advice from a person somewhere. The association simply serves as a broker for connections among organizations and enterprises across the state....

Another recommendation from both task forces was that there ought to be research parks developed in Illinois. As it happened, independently, the University of Illinois in Chicago had developed a notion that there ought to be one on the near West Side of Chicago, right next to the campus. And so the Chicago Technology Park developed. There was a plot of about fifty-six acres there that was partly vacant and ready for redevelopment (or decay). We thought we ought to make use of the strength of the medical center district nearby, an area that houses a number of the largest health-profession-related institutions in the region—or the country, for that matter....

We have in the park about an $8.8-million, state-funded incubator building we are just starting to fill up with tenants. We signed the first leases a few weeks ago. This is a state-of-the-art biological basic science research building, with "coldrooms," special water facilities, and the like. We have a private developer building intended to house medium-sized businesses. It is a place to which the new incubatees can graduate once they begin to grow. We have a major local Chicago company interested in establishing a major R&D facility within the park. We had one of our first incubatee successes long before we even had the incubator in place: we stuffed one of the faculty members of our local institution into an old, abandoned church there, and he proceeded to establish a company called Cell Analyses, which has now gone public, has moved out of the park, has about sixty or seventy employees, and is now making money. This shows that even in the Midwest, it can be done—culture or no culture!

The State of Illinois has established a set of technology commercialization centers on university campuses around the state. They are intended to couple not so much the scientific and engineering resources of the campuses as the *business*-related ones....You can get help there if you have a business idea. Whether you are a faculty member of that institution or not, you can get help with all the things you need to do to create a new business. It's been observed that the typical biochemist or physicist doesn't know much about venture capital or about writing a business plan or about providing security in a laboratory or the like. You can get help in this sort of thing from the university through the technology commercialization centers.

Resembling the technology commercialization centers is something we call the Illitech fund, which makes available seed capital to university investors to further their R&D on projects that have support from industry. One feature of that program is the matching of state funds to industry funds, which tends to bring the industries in at an early stage in the game and helps early on to promote the transfer of ideas in new technology. At the moment, at the University of Illinois in Chicago, we have funded by the Illitech Fund an image-recognition system, an ovulation prediction device, therapy-monitoring treatment of rheumatic diseases, and a device for testing the biological efficacy of stored blood.

One last enterprise I would mention is Access Illinois and the Illinois Resource Network. Sometime ago the University of Illinois established a a computerized data base that catalogs the faculty members and their R&D expertise throughout the universities in the state, both public and private. We now have a project underway at the University of Illinois in Chicago in cooperation with Illinois Bell and funded by Illinois Bell to create, if you will, the inverse: a catalog of all Illinois industries, with descriptions of the technology on which the industry depends and the technological needs of that industry....

Anthony Ponter:

We have an AMC (Advanced Manufacturing Center) at Cleveland State. There is also the Center for Automation and Intelligence Systems Research, the Edison technology center at Case Western, and the United Technology Center at Cuyahoga....

In July 1964 the Edison program provided $4.1 million to be distributed among the three institutions, the funding having to be matched by industrial contribution. At the outset, it was decided that Case Western would spearhead the basic research activities in the areas of artificial intelligence, expert systems, and automation systems control. It was also felt there was going to be a need for specialized training and retraining. Also, it was envisioned that a facility should be established wherein an awareness and use of new manufacturing and management technologies could be demonstrated; thus, the Cuyahoga Community College's role was directed to training and applying technology on the floors of the factories of this area. Cleveland State University's role pertained to applied research and technology development....

First, we had to solicit support from our industrialists to become sponsors of the programs as members. Being members entails such benefits as membership in the research steering committee, core research patent rights, etc. Membership costs $25,000 per annum for three years....

In launching these advanced manufacturing centers, first of all, nine faculty members from the electrical, mechanical, and industrial engineering departments submitted successful research proposals and proof of funding by the town council....I didn't want to set up something that would be obsolete in 5-10 years. That's destructive to careers in universities. A program is much more buoyant if you have colleagues coming from a department and going into manufacturing for a while, and making a contribution, and then returning back to their own department.

Shortly afterward, the director of the advanced manufacturing center was appointed, a man who was previously in charge of manufacturing technology at GE. Again, we had to decide whether to go with an academic or an industrial type. Of course, this is always of great interest to our senior colleagues in the universities. We wanted someone who would give us a window, I suppose, between us and Cleveland industries, someone with great technical expertise, and someone who would be able to garner the faculty's willingness to undertake a new role....

Some of our successful ventures were in production machinery performance and manufacturing operations. Since 1985, we have had twelve Edison-supported core projects—the original nine plus three that were supported last year. Last year we had to turn away $900,000 worth of work because of limited numbers of faculty and staff!

Lynn Berger

Community colleges across the country are playing an increasingly vital role in job training and economic development. In Illinois, the community college system is an integral part of the state's economic development efforts as a key partner with government, labor, and business not only to train and educate people for jobs but also to create and retain jobs. The Illinois mode involves funding and leadership at the state level as well as a wide variety of locally directed activities. The cornerstone is a network of business centers and economic development offices operated by all of Illinois' thirty-nine districts. These business centers are currently funded with a $3.7-million state appropriation for economic development grants. The intent of the grants is to enable every district to operate a business center or economic development office, to provide training and services to business, and to assist with local economic development efforts....

The economic development grants started four years ago with a $2.5 million state appropriation, which has increased annually with the significant results the program is showing. In fiscal 1986, under a $3.5 billion appropriation, the community college economic development efforts assisted 5,000 businesses in creating and retaining nearly 18,000 jobs. A wide variety of activities contributed to these efforts. A key activity in which every district is involved is customized job training for area business and industry. Whatever the subject matter, the college can design or broker a training program to fit the bill. Programs have even been offered at midnight or around the clock to serve industrial shifts. The training is provided under contract between the business and the college to train new employees or to retrain existing employees to keep them up to date or give them new skills. In many cases, the training is provided to assist with retraining or locating a company in the state. For example, Thornton Community College, just South of Chicago, in conjunction with the trainer from Ford Motor Company, recently developed and provided training in statistical quality control that enabled the local steel company to remain in business. That company had received many notices from companies for which it was a supplier that it was going to lose its contract unless it implemented ESCU measures. So, thanks to the ESCU training, the company was able to retain its contract and remain in business, and it also received the Outstanding Supplier Award from Allied Automotive Corporation in recognition of its on-time delivery and product quality....

The colleges also regularly help businesses seek funding for training through various state programs, which together provide over $20 million annually for training, as well as through the Job Training Partnership Act. But the vast majority of the training is paid for by the company itself....

All of the community college districts were involved in industrial development in the last fiscal year, and these efforts assisted in the attraction and expansion of nearly 200 companies and in the retention of sixty-eight companies, creating and retaining 5,000 jobs.

In addition to these activities, community colleges are also involved in a number of more innovative efforts to help small and large businesses. For example, many of them provide contract procurement consulting services to their area businesses that are interested in competing for state and federal contracts. This help can range anywhere from an introduction to the state and federal buying system to specific information and assistance on submitting bids. Currently, twenty-five of the thirty-nine districts provide such assistance to area business; seventeen of them devote a full-time person to this effort. In only three months' time, at the beginning of the current fiscal year, these seventeen full-time staff people helped generate $40 million in contracts for Illinois firms, topping the $32 million generated the entire previous year. As of the end of December, six months of effort helped generate $50 million in contracts. That's twice the goal for the entire year, so they're much more successful than we anticipated....

A number of community colleges are helping to establish labor management councils....The councils enhance local labor management relations, improve the local business climate, and create and retain jobs. Danville Area Community College established the first labor management council in the state over ten years ago. Recently, that labor management council worked with a local economic development corporation in retaining an industry that was being sold. The buyer was so pleased with the labor management relations in the plant and in the community that it decided to maintain its operation in Danville rather than relocate the plant. That would not have happened without the existence of the labor management council. This one effort retained over 250 jobs, and over the last few years, the retention and creation of thousands of jobs in Danville has been attributed to the existence of that one labor management council.

Increasingly, community colleges are also becoming involved in small business incubators, facilities that help new businesses get on their feet by providing low market rent, shared business services (such as secretarial, copying, telephone and accounting services, and employee training and management assistance).

Another emerging area for community colleges is the operation of advanced technology centers, not only to train the students on state-of-the-art equipment, but also to provide the use of that equipment to businesses and to assist with technology transfer....

Donald Holt

....Certainly, both public and research-oriented universities are awakening to their potential as tools for economic development. That makes sense because the major economic resources of any state or nation are its human capital, technology, biophysical capital, and institutional structure. Universities are intimately involved in either the production or maintenance of all of those various basic resources. Universities are particularly closely involved with agriculture. The land-grant universities in many ways have served as the R&D arm for production agriculture. It's important, as we try to deal with the problem of this so-called agricultural crisis and farm debt, to understand how that research and development system works. It is unique and has been extremely successful.

Basic and early-stage developmental research leading to new agricultural technology is conducted primarily by agricultural scientists of the USDA, the Agricultural Experiment Station, and the cooperative extension services. Private firms do most of the specific product development research that leads to new input products for agriculture, such as varieties, fertilizers, etc. Then the public institutions and agencies come back into the picture to test and compare the input products of agriculture to integrate those products into overall operational, profitable production, and marketing systems and to transfer the technology either indirectly or directly. By virtue of having the role of doing the applied research and transferring the technology, the university has a unique relationship with farming as an industry, compared with its relationship to many other industries.

The University of Illinois at Urbana-Champaign is helping to strengthen the linkages between the basic and early-stage developmental research programs in agriculture and other areas, and economic development. First, at the university scale, we recently created a position called "Director of Corporate Relations in Community Development." The director's first job is to orchestrate the development of a University of Illinois

Research Park at Urbana-Champaign. He has an associate director, whose primary responsibility is small business development in the Urbana-Champaign area. The college of agriculture at the University of Illinois is now implementing an incubator program designed to link our early-stage research efforts more closely with private-sector research, thus linking the institution more closely to economic development. The objective is to speed the commercialization of useful technology that originated in our programs.

The college is active in a number of promising areas, as is the whole institution. We have 125 scientists at Champaign who might be classified as biotechnologists, a large number of whom are in the college of agriculture. We are involved in supercomputers....We are also into artificial intelligence; in fact, that is the primary thrust of a number of our faculty members, and it concerns all the various aspects of artificial intelligence: natural language interfaces, image processing, and expert systems....

We also have another very important activity: the Value-Added Initiative. This is being enabled by an additional increment of $500,000 in recurring state funds to the college of agriculture to focus on value-added activities in agriculture, primarily on things that might help us utilize greater quantities of basic agricultural commodities that we produce in Illinois—namely, corn and soybeans....

The people of Chicago, a historically agricultural city, stand to benefit greatly from value-added research and development. But they will benefit only if production agriculture in Illinois can compete profitably and effectively in the international agricultural economy: otherwise, it won't matter how effective we are in developing new products that can be made from corn and soybeans or other agricultural commodities (though the potentials are great). It won't do the people of Chicago, or the people of Illinois, or the farmers of Illinois any good unless the farmers can be competitive in producing the products, or raw materials for the products. We're dealing in a global economy where the capital needed to produce the new plants, facilities, and products can flow just as readily to Brazil and Argentina as to Illinois, and it will flow to the places where the raw materials are most plentiful, most reliable, of highest quality, and most reasonably priced.

Mary Clutter

...It's about time we made economic competitiveness one of our high priorities. People are curious about why NSF is interested in economic competitiveness, and I hear people ask me all the time, "How on earth does NSF relate to economic competitiveness?" I say, "If you don't understand why NSF should be involved in economic competitiveness, then you don't understand what economic competitiveness is all about." ...When we talk about economic competitiveness, we're talking about a knowledge-based economy. Probably most of us in this room understand what that means, and most of us understand that, more and more, our economy is becoming knowledge based. We're highly dependent on skilled scientists and engineers to develop the new ideas, to create the new knowledge that we need to be economically competitive not only in the local economy, but in the global economy....

The federal investment in R&D is critical to our competitiveness and has been increasing, especially in the Eighties. During the current Administration it's gone up quite a lot, but in the nondefense area, we leveled off in the early 1970s and haven't really gone up much since then. But in the defense areas, we've gone up quite a lot. Federal obligations for R&D at universities and colleges in this country as a percentage of all federal R&D are pretty small—only a few percent of the total. Despite the fact that this Administration has been investing more heavily in R&D, in terms of our colleges and universities, the investment has been falling off about 1 percent per year. We think that's a dangerous thing. The federal investment in the R&D plant, the facilities, the instrumentation, and the infrastructure of the universities was at a high point twenty years ago. It just crashed and has not gone up. On the other hand, if you look at the percent of our R&D investment in the military, I don't have to say any more....

Another issue we have to consider is our work force. We're going to depend more and more on highly trained scientists and engineers to keep us on top in a high-tech society. The United States is still on top in training scientists and engineers, but Japan is closing in, and so are some other countries....In terms of jobs available now and in the foreseeable future, the only ones that are increasing are those for scientists and for engineers. The total jobs for scientists and engineers is going up with no sign of diminishing, but for professional workers and other kinds of workers, the total jobs are falling off.

If we look in terms of what we have available to keep us competitive, we know that the 22-year-old population will drop in the 1990s. The number of kids majoring in science and engineering is also falling off, so we're going to have a shortfall somewhere in the mid-90s of close to 700,000 people trained as scientists and engineers....

If we look at foreign students in this country who are obtaining Ph.D.s, we see that around 55–58 percent of all engineering Ph.D.s go to students from foreign countries. In math, physics, and chemistry there are increasing numbers. The only specialty that isn't being dominated by foreign students is the life sciences. If you break out the life sciences into agriculture and medical areas, you'll find that 40 percent of the Ph.D.s in the agricultural sciences are earned by foreign nationals. Now, we are not saying we want to close our doors to foreign students. The point is that we're becoming more dependent in certain areas on foreign students. If those students were suddenly called home, we would have serious problems in this country....

It's clear to us in Washington and at the NSF that we've got to take some action. The action we can take at NSF is to try to support the training of scientists and engineers and to support the research needed to create new knowledge that, hopefully, will be transferred into the market place at some level....

Our first priority at NSF is to develop human resources and broaden science and engineering participation. Because the population of 22-year olds is going down in the mid-1990s, we're going to have to broaden participation in science and engineering. There is one way we can do that pretty quickly—that is to change the culture. But we can't change the culture quickly. If we could, our problems would be solved. If we could attract more women into science and engineering and more minorities, then we would have the numbers we need to put us at the leading edge in economic competitiveness....By the year 2000 one out of every three or our citizens will be a minority person. If we don't take steps now to educate that minority in leading technology, we're all going to have a real problem on our hands....

Steven Gage

...From 1975–80 the Midwest experienced healthy growth in federal R&D. But it has dropped dramatically from 19 to 4.8 percent on a compounded growth rate from 1980–85. What has happened? A major sector shift from a broad portfolio of investments in energy, environment, transportation, etc., on the part of the federal government—funds that would go to many companies in the Midwest versus the concentration of defense industries location in the coastal states. The coastal states now have moved from 6.5 percent up to 12.5 percent on a compounded basis. So really, over the last seven years, there has been an 8 percent compounded growth rate difference between growth in the coastal states and in the Midwest. This is a major policy issue and is now being addressed tentatively in Congress....

In federal R&D to universities, midwestern universities have fared a little better. They were basically on a par growth rate during the 1975–80 period (around 11 percent) and have been lagging the coastal states by a full two percentage points in the past five years. If, in fact, the funding base to the midwestern universities had been growing at the same 9.5 percent that the growth rate to the coastal universities had been growing at, that would amount to a difference of $320 million over that five-year period. Now, that's enough money to fight for here in the Midwest. It's not just the two percentage point difference; we're talking about real money.

In terms of federal R&D dollars returned per one thousand dollars of federal tax money, our tax money is collected, sent to Washington, then some of it gets sent back, but more of it gets sent somewhere else. For each $1,000 collected on the average across the country, $64 is returned to the states for federal R&D contracts. In the coastal states now, $85 is returned, versus $25 here in the Midwest. The range here in the Midwest goes from about $13 per $1,000, up to only $43. So there's three times more money going to the coastal states in R&D....

In industrial support for universities, the Midwest basically lags behind the coastal states about 3 percent....

What do these lagging investments in midwestern companies mean?...It is those entrepreneurs who leave the Honeywells, the Control Datas, just in the Minneapolis area, to form literally the hundreds of smaller companies that are fueling the development of the Twin Cities. It's those people who leave all of the other companies in the Route 128, Silicon Valley, Southern California corridors and start the new companies—those are the people who actually start new companies. It isn't university people, for the most part. Those individuals who leave large companies do it as much out of frustration as for opportunity—but we need to recognize that we need those people in order to lead to new job growth, to lead to new economic development. Maybe the defense industries don't pay taxes. But remember, their employees do, their wives do, and their kids do. Employees also pay property, sales, state, and local taxes, which lead to better schools, better roads, and a whole set of social amenities that build the infrastructure of a region. Employees also pay tuition for their kids to go to colleges and universities. So this tremendous infusion of extra money going into the coastal regions is putting us here in the Midwest at an increasing disadvantage.

What does lagging investment in midwestern universities mean? Faculty are being hired away; it's hard to recruit new faculty into many of the universities here. The whole stage is being set for a declining ability to compete for future R&D

dollars either on the part of our companies or on the part of our faculties. It's a vicious downward spiral that is self-perpetuating....

How can the Midwest respond? First, we need a clarion call to wake up and admit how badly we're being treated in terms of funding and to quit worrying about being criticized by our peers in the coastal states that we're not just following federal policy, that we're not just following the dictates, the peer review system, and all of the other things we get hit with when we raise the issue that we here in the Midwest are getting shortchanged on every measure in terms of federal R&D. All of the rules that have been set up are basically being circumvented by a massive reallocation of federal R&D dollars from the previous five years to the most immediate five years. We need to take collaborative action, we need to let Congress and sympathetic people in the Administration know that these trends have set in and are driving us further and further out of the competitive race.

Higher Education, Economic Development, and the South

Overview

The United States has entered a new era of global competition and falling world commodities prices. The southern region of the United States has been hard hit because its economic structure is vulnerable to the emergence of other nations as lower-cost producers of many of the region's key manufacturing, agricultural, and resource-based products.

The competitive advantages enjoyed by the region during its decade and a half of strong growth—including relatively low operating costs, a surplus labor force, federal and other government funds that supported the development of its industrial infrastructure—have in many cases been counterbalanced by those of other nations. Whereas the region industrialized much faster than the rest of the nation during the 1960s and early 1970s, it has recently lost jobs in its traditional manufacturing sector.

Major economic concerns of the region include:

•*Rural development.* In nearly every southern state, a simultaneous decline in both traditional manufacturing and agriculture has had severe consequences for rural areas. The region's more diversified metropolitan communities have done better because of the strength of their technology and service industries (such as electronics, aerospace, tourism, and business and financial services).

•*International trade.* The South has done relatively well in attracting foreign direct investment and increasing exports to foreign markets. However, on balance, international trade has hurt the region because many newly industrialized countries have developed competitive advantages in the South's important traditional manufacturing industries.

•*Technological development.* As the rate of technological changes accelerates, the development and application of new product and process technologies are increasingly important to a region's ability to foster emerging industries and renew existing ones. At present, the South's technological capacity shows some weaknesses in relation to other regions.

• *New business support.* Assistance in gaining access to needed capital, in developing marketing and management skills, and in technology application is needed to foster the growth of new firms, particularly those than can take advantage of the new opportunities opened up by today's changing economic environment.

• *Human resource development.* To address all the preceding concerns, the region must have a skilled and adaptable work force, from top managers to first-line technicians. Developing this work force, a key to the region's future, requires new, flexible education and training approaches from community colleges to flagship universities.

Many colleges and universities in the region are making a special effort to help industry adapt and to prepare their students for new economic realities.   The 1987 southern regional seminar sponsored by AASCU, SRI, NAMTAC, and EDA reviewed these efforts and explored what more could be done to help the region.

The Historical Role of Higher Education in the Economy of the South

Southern colleges and universities have traditionally played a strong role in assisting one of the region's key industries: agriculture. Some of the region's land-grant institutions and agricultural extension services have broadened their tradition of public service and assistance to include other industries and have developed networks of individuals skilled in issues relating to rural development. Yet in many ways southern higher education's role in economic development has differed from that of other regions. Although the region as a whole has many strong institutions, some parts of the region do not have the world-class research institutions that have spurred the type of new-business formation seen in such places as Boston, Silicon Valley, and Salt Lake City. On the other hand, consistent with the southern states' economic development practices, their extensive community college systems have played a major role in providing free training and other incentives for businesses to choose to relocate in the state.

One reason for the limited technological capacity of southern colleges and universities is the low level of public-sector resources historically devoted to higher education. The region's lower income levels and scarce government resources have often led to lower funding for public education. In addition, while institutions in other regions—particularly in California and the Northeast—benefited from the federal research dollars that sponsored the development of new technologies and applications during and after World War II, comparatively little of the military spending in the South went to research. Instead, war-time spending in the region went primarily to building or expanding military bases, and to more traditional industries, such as chemicals, munitions, and shipbuilding. While more recent federal spending has spurred growth in such areas as Florida and Huntsville, federal spending at the region's universities still lags behind the national average.

As a result of these economic trends, as well as other social and political ones, the South's higher education system emerged in the 1950s with a relative lack of technological capacity and, in some areas, a relative abundance of liberal-arts, teachers-, and religious colleges. Since that time, large-scale, targeted investments by some states and universities have helped balance the overall capacity of the region's higher education system. For example, North Carolina's strong commitment since the 1950s to develop its high-technology infrastructure has both strengthened its Research Triangle universities and developed an important infrastructure outside its universities. Institutions such as Georgia Tech and the University of Texas at Austin have further demonstrated the ability of southern institutions to help meet the technological needs of both new and more traditional industries.

However, even given these efforts, spending on research and development in southern universities lags behind that in other regions. In 1982, total per-capita spending on research and development in universities in the United States was

$31.50, yet only $19.50 in the South. In that same year, per-capita industry R&D in universities stood at $1.40 for the United States, but only $1.23 for the South. However, there is great variation across the region; in Georgia both total and industry R&D spending (per capita) were well above the regional average, at $30.20 and $2.90, respectively.

Other factors have diverted state funds away from the development of balanced higher education systems that can play a broad role in supporting economic development. In some southern states the highly fragmented and politicized nature of higher education policy led to the proliferation of community and technical colleges, hence the region's relative strength in technical and occupational training. In addition, a focus on expanding enrollments rather than improving educational quality and institutional performance often stifled innovation and the willingness to reach out to local business.

As recognition of the importance of higher education in economic development has grown in recent years, all of the southern states have responded by devoting new funding and attention to their colleges and universities. Efforts have included developing a more comprehensive approach to higher education policy, funding centers of excellence and endowed chairs in specific research fields, and developing closer ties with local and regional industries. In making these efforts, many institutions are faced with the question of how they can best contribute to economic development given limited resources and, in many cases, a relatively weak capacity in many technological areas.

Recent Responses from Southern Higher Education

An array of innovative linkages for economic development have appeared among the region's colleges and universities. They are clearly important mechanisms in helping the region's economy adapt to new global economic realities. They are, by and large, pilot initiatives—the first attempts to come to grips with an entirely new competitive environment. To have a major impact on regional competitiveness, these initiatives must be replicated, expanded, or otherwise institutionalized. Other initiatives will no doubt also need to be adopted. But it is not clear what the next step should be. The 1987 southern regional seminar presented a forum for discussing next steps and determining the appropriate role of higher education in helping the region grapple with its problems and build on its strengths.

The recent breadth of college and university response to the region's economic needs has been impressive. For each issue, there are prime examples of what higher education can do to bolster a region's competitiveness.

Rural Development

Many colleges and universities in the South have begun to respond to the development needs of their communities in new ways. In some cases, this has meant providing assistance to prospective businesses in rural areas, or performing research and technical assistance on other issues—such as education, environmental protection, or local culture and history—pertaining to rural areas. Some prime examples of this kind of community capacity-building by higher education include:

• *Western Carolina University's Center for Improving Mountain Living.* Western Carolina University is involved in a number of economic development activities, but it has a distinct location for programs relating primarily to rural/mountain development in its Center for Improving Mountain Living. The center has four divisions that deal with issues relating to rural development: economic development, human resources, international programs (through which assistance is provided to other developing nations), and natural resources. In addition, the center hosts an organization called Western North Carolina Tomorrow (WNCT). Now six years old, WNCT was formed as a leadership structure to encourage active participation in the development of western North Carolina. Its activities have included the formation of a local venture capital intermediary (Venture Focus) and a high-technology subcommittee that has explored the potential of transferring federally owned technology to local private-sector firms.

•*Auburn University's Small Business Incubator Program.* The incubator program is a joint effort between Auburn University's Cooperative Extension Program (CES), its college of business, and the state's network of Small Business Development Centers. Begun in 1986, the effort focuses on assisting new business growth in communities that are not entitlement cities under the Community Development Block Grant (about 80 percent of which are rural). Federal funding supports the administration of the program in the CES, as well as the technical assistance to be provided to both incubator managers and their tenants through the CES and the state's Small Business Development Centers. The State of Alabama is providing funds to assist with the acquisition and renovation of incubator facilities.

International Trade

Recently, much attention has been focused on the need to understand foreign cultures, languages, and markets in order to compete successfully in the new global economy. The following institutions are among the southern colleges and universities that have responded to concerns about international trade:

•*Georgia Institute of Technology's International Trade Development Center* (ITDC). In 1979, a survey of Georgia businesses revealed that firms in the state had little knowledge of opportunities in international trade. In response, Georgia Tech started the ITDC, the initial function of which was to raise awareness of resources available in the state. Since then, its efforts have been expanded. The center now provides one-on-one counseling to firms showing strong export potential. It has also developed an export information system available to business clients within Georgia or to those in other states working with their local Small Business Development Center. The system provides firms with market information about foreign countries to enable them to explore potential markets for their products. Relationships with institutions in other countries have expanded the ITDC's information base; for example, through an exchange program with Stirling University in Scotland, the center can now obtain market information on European nations for any of its clients.

• *The University of South Carolina at Columbia's Master's Program in International Business Studies.* The International Business Studies program provides students with specialized knowledge needed to deal with international companies and business people. The two-year program's special approach includes an intensive language program and an overseas internship in addition to the traditional courses in management and international business. In their first year, students select a particular language track in one of six areas that include Japanese, Arabic, and French. In their second year, students take an internship (from 6–18 months) in the country or region of their specialization to strengthen their language skills and gain work experience in that region. In addition to the two-year master's program, special continuing education courses in export promotion and other topics relating to international business are also offered.

Technology Development and Transfer

The region's higher education system has played a key role in technological development, either through pioneering research at its major research universities or through its many strong technology transfer and assistance programs. However, because of increasing competitive pressure from other nations, the region must develop and—perhaps most important—*apply* new technologies faster than ever before. Programs such as those listed below exemplify higher education's most recent efforts to develop the South's capacity in the areas of technology development and transfer.

• *Georgia Institute of Technology's Georgia Technology Research Institute.* The Georgia Technology Research Institute includes seven major laboratories that work on industry and government-sponsored research projects. One of these laboratories is the Economic Development Lab, which houses the EDA University Center, the Georgia Productivity Center, and several types of technical assistance programs, and operates an industrial

extension service with twelve field offices across the state.
•*Haywood Technical College's High Technology Center*. The center, formed in 1985, has already shown a high degree of collaboration with local industry. In developing the plan for the center, more than 250 area businesses were surveyed about their greatest needs in high technology. As a result, the school's programs include a research center on new technologies and a demonstration center for new automated equipment that local firms can use in learning about new technological developments, as well as training courses that enable students to work on some of the most advanced flexible manufacturing and CAD/CAM training equipment available in the region.
•*North Carolina State's Industrial Extension Service*. As is true in many other southern states, NC State's Industrial Extension Service (IES) has been providing technical assistance to firms in the state for more than twenty-five years. In providing this assistance, the IES draws on expertise in a number of engineering fields, seeking to evaluate "soft" technologies (such as design modifications) as well as hard (new automated or flexible manufacturing processes) in finding a solution that can best meet the competitive needs of its clients.

Human Resource Development
The new global economy requires a broader understanding of other cultures, an ability to react quickly to market changes, and a capacity to learn new technologies. In short, industry needs a skilled and adaptable work force. In response to recent trends, colleges and universities in the region have begun to adapt current programs and introduce new initiatives with this aim in mind:
•*Auburn University's Engineering Outreach Program*. Recognizing that firms in more remote areas often have difficulty recruiting engineers who cannot find local opportunities for continuing education, Auburn University developed the Engineering Outreach Program, which allows students to be enrolled in Auburn's regular master's program in engineering while working in other parts of the state. Students attend

47

classes by viewing taped versions at home or at a local site, and turn in assignments to the same professor teaching the class at the university. They are also required to spend one semester taking a full course load on campus. In addition to enrolling students in the master's program, the outreach program provides training films to employers across the state.

• *Chattanooga State Technical Community College's Center for Productivity, Innovation, and Technology.* Founded in 1984, the center is believed to be one of the most sophisticated, state-of-the-art automation training facilities at any two-year college in the nation. In addition to providing training and re-training in some of the most advanced production techniques, the center also places a strong focus on training well-rounded technicians who have strong communication as well as technical skills. The curriculum for its associate degree program, therefore, includes courses on public speaking, technical writing, industrial psychology, and basic theory, as well as the traditional applied course work.

New-Business Support

It is increasingly evident that the formation of new businesses will be critical in maintaining regional employment, particularly in rural areas. However, the failure rate among new firms is quite high. Clearly, it is in the South's best interest to see that its entrepreneurs and new businesses receive the assistance they need to prosper, be it financial, managerial, or technological. Several colleges and universities have begun to address this need:

• *Georgia Institute of Technology's Advanced Technology Development Center* (ATDC). Founded in 1980 as an incubator to link university resources with new, technology-based industries, the ATDC now provides over fifty firms in the Atlanta area with an integrated set of services designed to support new companies during their first few years. Available on-site assistance includes help with business planning and management, as well as an incubator/innovation center that provides office, R&D, laboratory and light manufacturing space to new firms. In addition, through ATDC, firms can gain access to the equipment   and capabilities of the university for contract research, and contacts in the   local business community for help with more specific accounting, legal, and   financial assistance.

•*Texas A & M University's Institute for Ventures in New Technology.* The institute provides a variety of services to inventors and entrepreneurs,   including evaluation of technical feasibility, potential markets, production costs, and financial viability. Although it does not provide incubator   facilities, the institute does play a critical role in helping to hone ideas,   developing business plans, and providing a bridge between investors and inventors. As payment for its services, the institute receives an equity share   of its successful ventures.

Agenda

Southern Regional Seminar
April 27-28, 1987
Orlando, Florida

Opening General Session: Perspectives on the Economy of the South and the Role of Higher Education in Future Economic Development
Moderator: Stuart Rosenfeld, Director, Research and Programs, Southern Growth Policies Board
Presenters: Robert Kronley, Senior Consultant, Southern Education Foundation; Sheila Tschinkel, Senior Vice President and Director of Research, Federal Reserve Bank of Atlanta

Welcoming Address
Trevor Colbourn, President, University of Central Florida

Seminar Overview: The Higher Education-Economic Development Connection
Presenter: Theodore Lyman, Associate Director, Center for Economic Competitiveness, SRI International

Panel Discussion: College and University Programs Addressing Economic Issues in the South
Moderator: Beverly Milkman, Deputy Director, Grants Programs, Economic Development Administration
Panelists: Merton Cregger, Director, Center for Improving Mountain Living, Western Carolina University; David Clifton, Director, Economic Development Laboratory, Georgia Institute of Technology; James Hefner, President, Jackson State University; Leslie Ellis, Director, Office of Research Park Affairs, University of Central Florida; Jeffrey Tennant, Florida Atlantic University

Concurrent Workshops: Rural Development and the Dual Economy, Education and Training for a New Economy, Developing New Infrastructure, International Trade, Linking Technology with Economic Development

Luncheon Program
Remarks by Frank Hersman, Council of State Governments

Concurrent Workshops Continued

Closing Remarks
Steven Waldhorn, Director, Center for Economic Competitiveness, SRI International

Excerpts

Stuart Rosenfeld:

The Southern Growth Policies Board is a regional organization representing twelve southern states and Puerto Rico. Our chair is always a governor.... About a year and half ago, Governor Clinton of Arkansas, our last chair, appointed the 1986 Commission on the Future of the South. There were four conditions central to the environment in which the commission began its work. First, the disparities between the urban and rural areas were increasing. The South still lags behind the rest of the nation on most indicators of well-being. It has moved close to the U.S. average, but averages can be deceiving: you've heard about the statistician who sat with his head in the oven and his feet in the refrigerator and said that the average felt pretty good. There's a great deal of variation within the rural areas, but the rural areas are still well below the urban areas.

For example, in 1981 per-capita income in the United States was $10,500. Southern urban per-capita income was just about the same, southern rural per-capita income was $7,700, and southern rural black per-capita income was $3,200. At the end of 1985 the urban unemployment rate in the South was down to just over 6 percent, but nonmetropolitan counties were still at almost 10 percent. The same is true for literacy rates. Adult literacy rates based on people with no more than an eighth-grade education in the metro areas is 20 percent and in the rural areas 30 percent. Leaders were aware that there was a shortage of jobs in the South, that many of the jobs we'd gotten in the past hadn't been good jobs, and that many southerners are not prepared for the new jobs. Rural economic activity was most successful in areas of the South where costs were lowest, where education was weakest, and where a docile surplus labor force existed. Human resources were measured by quantity, not quality. Incomes rose mostly because they were so low originally. There were more people entering the work force—two people in a lot of families. And, paradoxically, success in smoke-stack chasing, which has been the way we attracted jobs, was predicated on failure to achieve success. Therefore, the dispari-ties between urban and rural areas and between the races is increasing in the South.

The second condition the commission examined was the change in the region's economy from a manufacturing base to a service base. People refer to the Midwest as America's indus-trial heartland, but the South, and particularly the rural South, is highly dependent on older, traditional manufacturing indus-tries. Three out of every ten people employed in the rural South are operators, fabricators, or laborers, and these industries are declining. They don't generate the large unemployment lines to make the national news, but they add up to a serious problem....

Third, competition is becoming global rather than regional. And the new job war is with other countries, not other states. We knew how to compete with other states and other regions: we'd just provide more incentives or a better business climate. But we don't have that freedom with countries who don't operate under the same ground rules we do....

Fourth, the federal government is no longer there to help when we need it.

For the work of the Commission on the Future of the South, Governor Clinton made it clear he wanted a very different kind of report from those of the past. He wanted one written for the public, one that was meant to be read rather than to decorate bookshelves. He wanted something that could be *implemented.*

The commission divided itself into three committees: hu-man resource development, technology and innovation, and governmental structure. Economic development was funda-mental to the purpose of the board and the theme that linked everything together. The commission agreed that its overarch-ing concern was raising per-capita income in the region and getting people out of poverty and into self-sufficiency. With that in mind, the commission identified concerns that transcend all these main issues, such as quality of life, equity, and urban rural concerns, as well as internationalization of infrastruc-ture....

We brought together the heads of all the high-tech authorities people concerned about technology to see what we might be able to do cooperatively. As a result of that meeting, we developed the idea for a new subsidiary organization called the Southern Technology Council, created to facilitate technology transfer and development and to assess programs and to provide information to legislative people working in technology transfer. Twelve states joined initially, and each governor appointed two members to the council....

When the council met for the first time to map out a strategy, the most strongly expressed view was that it ought to produce tangible results—something more than paper or ideas. A proposal was made to find some way to improve the region's R&D capabilities and capacities through cooperation.... We received a grant from the Appalachian Region Commission to develop such a plan. The plan will identify the research strengths of the South and look for the potential markets and opportunities, and come up with some alternative strategies of working cooperatively, and an economic rationale in terms of jobs for accomplishing them. Hopefully we'll start to create some multistate centers. That's important to the universities and colleges that can't be leaders, that aren't going to draw big R&D dollars....

We're also examining automation. We want to identify state and local policies or programs that can encourage plants to modernize to invest in new technologies rather than shut down. Even if there will be fewer jobs, we need those jobs there. Colleges and universities are central to the state policies of providing advice and technical assistance, R&D, and computers. We're surveying seventy-five businesses that have already automated in the nonmetropolitan regions of the South. We're compiling a list of all of the technology-related activities going on in the South. We want to become a clearinghouse for technological development activities....

Sheila Tschinkel

Our region has to start the crucial process of improving our human resources so that we can start catching up economically or even start staying even, which we're not doing now, with the rest of the nation. We have to raise our level of technological awareness so that we can be economically innovative and can—and this is important—learn to grow our own businesses. We need to streamline our governments and our educational systems to generate a better environment for labor and business....

The Commission on the Future of the South has developed a ten-point program that we hope can help us catch up and participate in the future.... First, we want to provide a nationally competitive education for all southern students by the year 1992. This is probably the only recommendation that requires spending money. In the South we still spend 20 percent less per student than the national average. Less than 70 percent of ninth graders ever even graduate from high school. We cannot even contemplate having the labor force we need without better education.

Not unrelated to this was the next objective: to mobilize resources and eliminate adult functional illiteracy by 1992. The statistics on these are also very revealing. People who are functionally illiterate earn 44 percent less than those who have a high school education. One in four southern adults never went beyond the eighth grade. For blacks the number is one in three. Functional illiterates are likely to be more dependent on welfare and involved in crime. If southerners are going to be able to participate in the economy of the future, and even in the current one, we must improve public education today, and we also have to help those whose education was stunted in the past.

Of course, if you do the first two things, you're part of the way to creating a flexible and globally competitive work force by 1992. Our business and labor must be able to compete with those in the rest of the nation and also with those in the rest of the world.

Vocational education needs to be revamped. Workers have to obtain skills that are portable. I'm not so sure we have to train people with particular skills as if we could predict what particular jobs they were likely to hold in the future. We have to give them the basics so they can learn a new job when their present job changes. It might be a good idea to make community colleges responsible for federal vocational funds because they're there and because we may have built too many colleges all over the South, particularly when enrollments are likely to decline....

We need to conserve these educational resources and increase the South's capacity to generate and use technology. We have fewer engineers and physicists and other applied scientists in the South, so we need to upgrade our own local graduate programs in science and technology. We can create state and regional centers of excellence. We may not need as many local centers as we have; it's just too costly to fragment and respond to individual factions, particularly when there is likely to be less and less money available to do things we need to do. We need to encourage technology and economic innovation. We have to implement economic development strategies to generate a home-grown economy that is viable....

The commission also focused on the need to improve our human resources; generally, we have to reduce the numbers of families at risk, and then we have to enhance our own natural and cultural resources. We cannot keep or retain business if our quality of life is poor.

Another factor the commission thought crucial is leadership. We need pragmatic leadership with a global, not local, vision. We need to start building and strengthening leadership at every level of government in the South. In many cases this starts with the schools. After all, it's difficult to lead people any further than you've gone yourself. If we do this, it will help improve the structure and the performance of state and local government. In many cases we have state and local government structures left over from the last century. We cannot cope with less and less federal aid unless we learn to economize at the government level and promote interdependence instead of factionalism....

Robert Kronley

The Southern Education Foundation for 120 some years has been concerned with equity in education. Our interest in this area, particularly education and economic development, and even more particularly higher education and economic development, is in stimulating policies and programs that result in equity....

There is little significant, sustained interaction between and among private foundations and our educational institutions. That's a problem and a shame. Philanthropic entities can do a lot to stimulate economic development activities through our higher education institutions. They can provide seed grants to support models that can be developed and perhaps replicated elsewhere; they can link together parties with specific interests; they can support several kinds of research. But one of the reasons foundations have only been active in this sporadically is that they are wary of risk....

They are also limited in funding. The kind of investment needed by our higher education institutions to help stimulate their active and sustained involvement in economic development activity is very, very expensive, and for a foundation like the Southern Education Foundation, our average grant is only something like $12,000. For foundations like the Ford Foundation, which give away a lot more money and have much higher average grants, there are other investments that seem more malleable and more interesting. These things may, in fact, affect economic development although they are not seen that way-early childhood education, rural educational enhancement, supply and quality of teachers, the effects of the educational reform movement on people who are not caught up necessarily in the debate about excellence, people who are poor....

We're working now on something called "The Fund for Rural Educational Enhancement," which we have called "FREE," although the only thing free about it is its name. FREE is supposed to stimulate involvement in education through the creation of local funds. There is a great model for this in urban areas. There are forty-five of them situated throughout the United States in cities. They've attracted a good deal of community and citizen interest in involvement in local educational activities. They raise money, and they distribute it in a way that enhances activities in schools....

The Southern Education Foundation created a task force in education and economic development to advise the foundation on what it could do to stimulate programs at postsecondary institutions, and to make general recommendations to the institutions themselves. We conducted case studies of six postsecondary education institutions in the South, which were not normal selections for such kinds of studies. We chose a flagship institution, two four-year, predominantly white institutions, and three small black colleges, two public and one private. The case studies revealed that even among institutions more actively involved in this area, the process of promoting economic development was not really perceived by the actors themselves. There were few administrators, and, frankly, even fewer faculty members who did accept the notion that there ought to be a prolonged involvement, almost part of an institutional mission, in terms of economic development on the part of the institution. At the same time there was a notion that there was really no relationship between that kind of activity and the economic and social health of the community of the institutions. Programs at these institutions grew up almost unanimously as a result of an individual faculty person, usually through one grant, rather than out of a deliberate or planned institutional structure.

There are several reasons why these institutions will not undertake sophisticated efforts in economic development. The first applies to both the private and public sectors: lack of inspired leadership. Administrators simply refuse to look at the symbiotic relationship between institutional growth and community development, and even when they do, they aren't sure about effective ways of participating. Second is a simple lack of administrative expertise. In the six schools we looked at, five had to go outside the schools and hire nonteaching professionals to manage economic development activities. Once they did this, they became divorced from what was perceived as the mainstream of the institution. Third was lack of funds. Fourth was internal resistance: faculty and staff members had done it their way for many years, it was "not their job," and they simply did not want to get involved....

Beverly Milkman

There are a number of different ways a university can become involved in economic development. Certainly, a university's basic mission is human resource development. It certainly is a major contributor to the economic development area, but it doesn't happen to be the kind of economic development that EDA funds because we view that as part of the university's basic mission anyway, and something it should automatically be doing and trying to improve.

Other areas of assistance universities can provide are small business development. Funding small business development centers is an area that EDA as an agency is starting to move away from, not because we don't think it's important, but because there is a very large Small Business Administration program that is funding these kind of centers, and there's also a minority business development agency, which funds organizations that work with minority small businesses. So, we at EDA began looking for another area. After we had gotten these other activities started, we said, Is there anything else we should be doing? Some of our centers all along had concentrated on working with community-based groups and with small towns, counties, multicounty districts in providing services to the public and quasipublic sectors. That is a trend EDA is now focusing on, particularly university centers that are going to work with the public and the nonprofit communities....

Merton Cregger

With few exceptions, the rural areas of the United States are in a decline. That decline is perhaps most pronounced in the Southeast. Worldwide economic trends are principally the cause of this decline, but it is also caused by the lack of a coherent and effective strategy for rural development....

When you do away with the rhetoric, the only strategy in place at present in the rural areas, at the national and the state level, is that of urbanization, of extending development along the interstates, of concentrating services in the metropolitan areas, of turning hamlets into towns and towns into cities, and of benign neglect, particularly by the federal government. It seems that it is high time that priority be given to reversing this trend of rural deterioration....

Western Carolina University has taken up the challenge. Its setting is indeed rural. Established in 1889 as a normal school, it is situated on farm land some seven miles from the nearest town. The university was deliberately set there by its founder because he reasoned that if education was to be brought to the mountains, it had to be given in the mountains for people from the mountains. The school has grown over the years from a normal school to a comprehensive, regional one today. The concentration of its service area is in the mountain counties in the western part of our state. It is one of the sixteen member universities in the North Carolina system.

Up until about fifteen years ago, WCU's mission was quite traditional, with heavy emphasis on teaching, not too much research, and a service program principally confined to continuing education. There was some international structure work going on in the area, and a school of business housed an EDA-funded economic development center. These activities were quite peripheral to the main concerns of the university, however. But the picture changed dramatically with the inauguration of Chancellor H. F. Robinson, who determined that the institution would more completely fulfill its role as a regional university through a greatly enhanced outreach and service program. The cultural, social, and economic needs of the mountain region were analyzed. Out of the analysis arose the mountain learning center, the biological research center, the Michael Computer Science Network, a program to upgrade two-year college faculty, a Cherokee center, the rural education center, and the Center for Improving Mountain Living (CIML)....

The work of the center is carried out through five divisions: economic development, leadership development, natural resource development, resource management, and international programs. This divisional organization reflects the problems and needs of our region....

The Center for Improving Mountain Living concentrates on helping *existing* industries and start-ups to develop within the region, as opposed to making extensive efforts to attract *outside* industries. Because our population is growing older, we are developing and concentrating on intergenerational programs. Our natural resource work is primarily in pollution prevention and toxic material handling because of the great fragility of our mountain ecosystems. We've also addressed the need for great leadership development. Over the last seven years we have been instrumental in the development and expansion of a seventeen-county leadership organization called Western North Carolina Tomorrow, or WNCT. This organization has become a viable and vital force in promoting regionalism, which is terribly fractured because of the mountainous character, and in providing a forum on critical issues that face the region. We also have an active program, in cooperation with the North Carolina Institute of Government, for training local government officials....

David Clifton

Georgia Tech is involved in economic development in almost every way a university can be. Our involvement with industry in economic development takes many forms.

Our industrial extension service offers a unique model that can be replicated at other universities. To look at the industrial extension service, we first have to look at the mission of economic development in the laboratory in which it's located. The lab achieved several goals in defining legislation by the Georgia Assembly, so the state legislators gave us a mission statements: to encourage further economic development, to provide technical assistance to business and industry, to encourage the more complete development and utilization of natural resources in Georgia, and to provide an industrial extension service....

The service, in addition to working with the companies, assists local and state economic development groups. A recent program was an economic research development program to look at a group of counties, a rural area, decide what their human and natural resources are, and then help target industrial opportunity in that area and identify which industries match that area's resources. At the same time, we'll do a survey of the manufacturers in that area, the economic development community in the area and the state, and give this multicounty area feedback on its strengths and weaknesses as other people view them, which is very useful....

Why do we have a successful operation? First, we were fortunate in earlier years to have an EDA university center grant that helped us get started. Second, in recent years, we've had a lot of state funding. Third, we've recognized that the bottom line for economic development programs is creating jobs, and that requires a team effort. A university can't do it all by itself....

James Hefner

Back at the beginning of the 1970s, the motto adopted by Mississippi was "75 by 75." The goal was to raise Mississippi's average per-capita income to 75 percent of the national average by 1975. It never happened. In fact, the closest the state ever came was 71 percent in 1976. Since then, the state's percentage has slowly declined. After hovering around 69 percent of the national average in the early 1980s, Mississippi's per-capita income has again begun dropping relative to other states in the past couple of years. The 1985 per-capita income figures show Mississippi at $9,035, or 67 percent of the national average....

During the past several years, the only growth in Mississippi has been in service jobs—mainly, in fast food outlets, which are among the lowest paying. In 1986, Mississippi lost some 3,000 jobs in durable goods while picking up 6,200 service jobs. Mississippi's average hourly earnings of production workers as of October 1985 were the lowest of any state in the South, at $7.26. Mississippi is first among all other southern states in the percentage of transfer payments.

Between 1981 and 1984, Mississippi had an estimated out-migration of 16,000 persons, second only to Kentucky's 36,000. Mississippi was significantly higher in all, but Tennessee was higher in the per-capita amount of state payments to local governments. At the same time, the amount of state and local government revenues received by Mississippi from the federal government at 23.4 percent was second highest in the nation and substantially higher than the national average.

In sum, the State of Mississippi desperately needs more higher-paying jobs. Progress in the municipal aspect just hasn't materialized much. Mississippi is still very dependent on the federal government to boost its economy.

In October 1986 Jackson State University satisfied a long-standing need in Mississippi by establishing an International Visitors Center. Although the center is located on the Jackson State campus, and its president and executive director are faculty members, it serves primarily the City of Jackson. Its funding comes directly from the state's department of economic development, the Jackson Chamber of Commerce, the county supervisor, and the city's convention centers. It has a modest budget of $60,000 in addition to the income benefits provided by the university....

Since October 1986, the center has hosted over a hundred visitors, from such countries as Nigeria, Denmark, the People's Republic of China, the Philippines, Egypt, Brazil, Great Britain, Argentina, Japan, Korea, West Germany, and France. Visitors have included engineers, planners, members of parliament, under-secretaries, and educators. The center relies on members of the board and volunteers to host the visitors....

Leslie Ellis

Let me tell you a little about the Central Florida Research Park, a university-related research park established as a result of enabling legislation passed in the Florida legislature in 1978. That legislation is not unique to to the University of Central

Florida, but applies to all the universities in the state university system of Florida. In that sense, we all operate on the same legislative basis when we decide to go about establishing a university-related research park.... The legislation requires involvement between a county or counties and a university if a university-related research park is to be established....

The ultimate goal of the park is to establish an academic industrial communityresulting in a unique approach to the creation of more effective and cooperative academic and industrial endeavors. We believe that the potential for the establishment of close ties between the university and industry will create an attractive environment conducive to the location of research-oriented industry in the park. This activity will enrich and support the university's teaching and research....

We formed a university and park long-range planning council, which meets regularly and addresses problems common to both the park and the university. We have developed a university and park joint-use relationship that provides for residents of the park campus parking privileges, campus services, and facilities, and campus and park communication links.... We have established an orientation program for faculty, administrators, and staff of the university. Individuals and groups are invited to visit the park to see its facilities and to hold their meetings there.... Currently, over 10 percent of the employees in the park are either undergraduate or graduate students, faculty consultants, part-time faculty and UCF graduates.... Currently, the park is administered by five employees, who are employees of the Orange County Research and Development Authority, and who report directly to me as chairman of the Authority. We have an executive director, a park manager, a director of marketing, an administrative assistant, and a receptionist. That number will increase in the near future....

Jeffrey Tennant

Florida Atlantic University is attacking economy development on a broad front. Our service to existing high-tech industry involves providing consultants, a great deal of research, and joint projects.

You may be familiar with the Florida High Technology Council, which provides approximately $12 million a year for joint projects between Florida industry and universities. We have a number of such projects. We provide a lot of information services to industry through the use of the university's own library, and we make them available to surrounding industry. We also operate the NASA-STAC (Southern Technology Applications Center) program, begun in Florida and now propagated to most of the states in the Southeast, and a major tool for assisting industry.

Certainly, our advanced graduate programs are a primary attractant to high-technology industry and to the service industry. They, in turn, serve us by providing communications, the political impetus for us to acquire those programs. We realize that if we're going to offer advanced graduate programs to business and industry, we must have them on a convenient schedule. We must have a faculty that is cooperative and sympathetic to the operation, and we do. We're pleased that our faculty is responsive to the needs of industry. We also make use of the State of Florida system, which involves videotape deliveries, of course, and is called FEEDS (Florida Engineering and Education Delivery System). Most of the engineering schools in the state university system participate in FEEDS, and up until a year ago, we were the primary provider of courses on that system. We offer them not only to the local area but also to the entire state. Other state university system schools provide courses in our area using this same system.

Certainly, these industries want access to our graduates in the professional areas. At the same time, we want to make them feel as though they're participating in shaping what those graduates look like in terms of their programs. We have an active program of advisory councils, committees, etc. for each of our academic programs in the technical and scientific areas to get the input from the major industries and make them feel as though they're playing a role in the development of the institution. You can imagine that that feeds back positively politically for us, in terms of gifts to our foundation and in terms of the direct input they give us....

Frank Hersman

The Council of State Governments (CGS) is one of three principal organizations that represent state government interests. The other two are the National Governors' Association and the National Conference of State Legislators. The other two groups are the political lobbying arms for state government, while CGS considers itself the professional research arm of state government.

The council's strengths lie in its regional activities. We have four regional offices, in New York City, Chicago, San Francisco, and Atlanta. Most regions have a regional governor's conference and a regional legislative conference.... In addition, CGS serves as an umbrella organization for some fifty separate organizations of state government .They involve the newer kinds of activities and associations of state government as opposed to the traditional activities. Examples include the National Conference of Lieutenant Governors, the National Association of State Personnel Directors, purchasing officials, probation and parole authorities, voting administrators, and secretaries of state....

CGS undertakes "cultivation" activity in the knowledge community and the state government community. We go to great lengths to cultivate credibility and trust. One way we do this is by developing new leadership activities that bring to the floor those people in state government who are going to try and attempt to change the dynamics of state decision making. We also give awards for outstanding examples of state activity so that the best models can be brought forward. We develop innovation reports on what is being done that's successful and not successful. In the knowledge community, we're also recognizing people who provide outstanding service to state governments. We've created a visiting scholars program to bring people in from the academic or other knowledge resource communities to invigorate the council's research and related activities. We are developing cooperative relationships with colleges and universities and private think tanks and training activities so that the work of those colleges or universities or training programs can be made more available and usable across the nation to the state government constituency we represent. The council offers national access to a broad range of state decision makers.

Some of the traditional program activities of CGS involve the development of model legislation. We disseminate this information in a biannual publication called *Suggestive State Legislation....* We have a national panel of about 100 leaders from state governments who give us some 500 suggestions annually on legislation and activities. We also produce information reports. We put out the typical standard reference books that relate to state governments; the flagship publication is a book called *The Book of the States.* We also put out a directory of all the people involved in different activities in the Executive, Legislative, and Judicial branches.

Recently, we've adopted a strategic plan for the council that involves five areas: education, economic development, health, environment, and public finance. That strategic plan is driving our research activities at present. We're also conscious, however, that the strategic plan is just the beginning of a planning and programming activity, so we're constantly trying to keep it alive and dynamic. Last week, for example, we brought together about 100 in state government from around the nation to consider the alternative futures of state government and what it would take to develop intervention strategies so that current conditions that were judged adverse might be improved....

Higher Education, Economic Development, and the Northeast

Overview

The United States has entered a new era of global competition. This change has affected the Northeast in different ways. In recent years, parts of the Northeast have thrived as a result of technological innovation and the growth of advanced business and financial services (e.g., eastern Massachusetts, northern New Jersey, southern New Hampshire). Other areas, however, have fallen behind because of their dependence on declining industries that have been slow to adjust to global competition (e.g., western Massachusetts, western New York, western Pennsylvania).

Whereas many regions look to their natural resource base for a unique comparative advantage, the Northeast relies on its abundant colleges and universities and highly educated work force as its primary assets. The recent resurgence of much of New England and parts of the Middle Atlantic states can be attributed in large measure to the region's skilled and adaptable work force. Higher education in the Northeast has played a key role in creating this comparative advantage.

Despite the economic revival of much of the region, the Northeast still faces a number of competitive challenges. The major economic concerns of the region include:

• *Maintaining technological leadership.* Even New England's fast-moving high-technology industries are being challenged as never before by competition from abroad. Other states and nations are investing in technological research that is instrumental not only in renewing today's industry but in developing tomorrow's new industry as well. As in the past, northeastern higher education has an important role to play in helping the region move toward the next level of technological innovation.

• *Supporting finance and service industries.* The last decade has witnessed an explosion of "advanced services" such as banking, investment counseling, business services, consulting, and the like. Several northeastern cities have become thriving service centers during that time. Today, however, as in manufacturing, foreign and domestic competition is challenging these industries as never before. Therefore, the region's advanced-service industries must adopt new technologies (telecommunications, software, and related innovations) and better understand new markets (both domestic and international).

•*Easing the transition of traditional manufacturing.* In addition to its high-technology and advanced-services strengths, the Northeast maintains an important base of more traditional manufacturing industry. Although declining, such industries as steel, metal working, and industrial machinery manufacturing are still the centerpieces of many local economies throughout the region. For these areas, the issues are much like those facing midwestern communities. State governments, through their universities, are attempting to help these industries regain their competitiveness through special research and technology transfer efforts.

•*Assisting distressed communities.* The economic resurgence of New England is a success story that has been well documented. Less publicized, however, is the fact that many rural and inner-city communities in the Northeast have not participated in this process of economic renewal. Dual "have/have-not" economies may be emerging in the region. To counter this trend, some colleges and universities have begun to reach out to the region's distressed communities.

•*Developing human resources.* To address all the preceding concerns, the region must have a skilled and adaptable work force, from top managers to first-line technicians. This has historically been the Northeast's greatest asset. But in today's highly competitive environment, new, flexible education and training approaches are required to maintain the region's comparative advantage.

Many colleges and universities in the region are making a special effort to help industry adapt and to prepare their students for new economic realities. Other institutions want to do more, but have not developed the capacity as yet. The northeastern regional seminar reviewed these efforts and explored what more could be done to help the region.

The Historical Role of Northeastern Higher Education in Economic Development

While other parts of the country have relied on their natural-resource base to provide a unique comparative advantage, the Northeast has relied on strong universities and a highly educated work force as its primary assets. These strengths have enabled the region's economy to evolve successfully from, for example, textiles to machine tools to computer manufacturing. From the colonial period, with an economy of small mills and shops for wood- and metal-working tools, farm equipment, production machinery, and textiles, the Northeast has been characterized by continual technological innovation. The 19th-century Industrial Revolution began in the Northeast because of the region's concentration of skilled craftsmen and entrepreneurs. The same elements have contributed to the region's resurgence 150 years later as it has moved into advanced manufacturing and computer-related development and production.

This is not to say that the Northeast has uniformly restructured itself to meet competitive demands. For example, while eastern Massachusetts, southern Connecticut, eastern New York, northern New Jersey, southeastern Pennsylvania, and southern New Hampshire have become thriving high-technology manufacturing or advanced-service centers, parts of western New York, western Massachusetts, northern Maine, and western Pennsylvania have been slow to adjust because of their continued reliance on hard-hit traditional industries such as steel, textiles, industrial machinery, and the like. Nevertheless, a highly skilled and adaptable work force continues to be the main reason for much of the region's recent revitalization. Higher education in the Northeast has been largely responsible for creating this comparative advantage.

The Northeast has always been a national leader in education. It provided the first university in America (Harvard in 1636) and the first system of free public education (Connecticut in 1642). Within the region, higher education is especially strong in the New England states. New England's 264 colleges and universities represent 10 percent of the nation's total, whereas the area's population represents only 5 percent of all Americans. Together, these states have 50 percent more colleges and universities per capita than the nation as a whole. They possess almost twice as many private institutions per capita as the rest of the country.

The Northeast not only has a high number of higher education institutions per capita, but overall quality as well. On nearly every indicator of educational excellence, the New England and Middle Atlantic states composing the Northeast are among the top performers in the country in terms of faculty quality, levels of R&D spending, research results, and educational attainment of the work force. Only the Pacific region exceeds New England in the quality of science and engineering faculty and published research articles per faculty member. New England leads the nation in patents issued per capita. The Middle Atlantic subregion—comprising the states of New York, New Jersey, and Pennsylvania—consistently ranks among the top three or four census regions on these indicators.

New England boasts the highest levels of total per-capita R&D and industry R&D expenditures in universities in the nation. The Middle Atlantic is again among the top three or four subregions in these categories. The New England and Middle Atlantic regions rank first and third, respectively, in science and engineering Ph.D.s per capita, and second and fourth in the percentage of their population with at least four years of college. As an indicator of the continuing importance of higher education, these subregions also rank first and third in the percentage of 16- to 24-year olds attending four-year colleges and universities.

The key to the Northeast's wave of technological innovation and economic renewal has been its talented and entrepreneurial work force. Higher education has always played the central role in human resource development, but not until after World War II did the region's colleges and universities become important contributors of applied research for industry and the federal government. In New England and, to a lesser extent, the

Middle Atlantic states, the scientific and business orientation of higher education grew substantially, with university-based research and development becoming a major source of revenue and economic spin-off activity. The 1950s and 1960s brought an aerospace and defense industry boom that injected large amounts of new R&D funds into many New England and some Middle Atlantic universities, enabling them to build up their general institutional capacity. Cutbacks in defense spending in the late 1960s and early 1970s disrupted this growth, but the seeds had been planted to produce the next wave of technological innovation and trained workers. Much of this activity took place in the region's private colleges and universities, which until the 1960s accounted for about three-quarters of the enrollment in New England's higher education.

While the region's private institutions prospered in the period after World War II, state systems of public higher education also emerged. A major expansion took place during the 1960s. Substantial state investments in higher education in New England, for example, increased enrollment in public colleges and universities from less than one-quarter to more than one-half of the region's total from 1960-1980. During this time, the public university system in New York grew to be one of the nation's largest, with satellite campuses throughout the state. Although private institutions have been and continue to be more important to this region than to any other, public institutions, by their size, dispersion, and various research strengths, have also become critical to the educational and technological leadership of the Northeast.

In some ways, public higher education in the Northeast may be even more important to the region than its private colleges and universities. Many of the region's private institutions are national not only in stature, but in focus as well. This fact has often meant limited attention to the region's particular economic or labor needs. Although many of these "national universities" have helped generate new industry in some areas (Harvard, MIT, and the Boston area, for example), their impact on older sectors of the economy (e.g., traditional manufacturing) and other parts of their states (e.g., western Massachusetts, western New York) historically have been limited.

In some cases, the benefits of top-level research and instruction have been lost as graduates have joined companies—and university findings have been applied—outside the region (e.g., despite Massachusetts' phenomenal job growth, nearly 30,000 left the state between 1980 and 1984, and companies throughout the country tapped its major universities for innovative research). Many of the region's private institutions are also prestigious liberal arts colleges and universities whose research and instructional strengths do not coincide with the immediate needs of industry.

Public institutions in the Northeast are more dispersed geographically (especially to rural areas with few higher education options) and tend to be more tailored to the needs of their local communities. Moreover, states throughout the country have also been much more active since 1980 in funding special industry-tailored research programs and in demanding more direct economic impact from their public colleges and universities. In recent years, state institutions in the Northeast have begun an array of new research and instructional programs aimed at helping their local economies more directly. New industry-university partnerships have emerged to address the needs of new and old industries alike. But these initiatives are only a beginning. Although some institutions have been entrepreneurial, others have been slow to progress.

Recent measures also show that the region's financial commitment to public higher education is not growing and, if anything, may be slipping. The Middle Atlantic ranks third, but New England ranks seventh of nine census regions on the level of total state and local education expenditures per capita. Looking more closely at these figures reveals that the problem is not with elementary and secondary education (the Middle Atlantic and New England subregions rank first and second nationally on per-pupil spending at this level), but rather with higher education. Seven of the nine northeastern states rank among the fifteen lowest in the nation in state and local expenditures per capita for public higher education.

In another dimension, whereas public colleges and universities in New England are responsible for about 50 percent of total higher education enrollment, they represent only about 30 percent of the total graduate student enrollment. In an era in which applied research and professional research-oriented education is critical to economic transformation, a good portion of the Northeast may not be fully realizing the potential of its graduate-level public higher education.

Despite these concerns, northeastern higher education, both public and private, has been more active in making the connection to regional economic development than ever before. As new economic challenges have emerged, colleges and universities have undertaken a variety of special initiatives.

Recent Responses from Northeastern Higher Education

A number of innovative linkages to economic development have appeared among the region's colleges and universities. These are clearly important steps in helping the region's economy adapt to new global economic realities. Most are pilot initiatives—the first attempt to come to grips with an entirely new competitive environment. If they are to make a major impact on regional competitiveness, these initiatives must be replicated, expanded, or otherwise institutionalized. Other initiatives will no doubt also need to be adopted, but it is not clear what the next step should be. The northeastern regional seminar presented a forum for discussing next steps and determining the appropriate role of higher education in helping the region grapple with its problems and build on its strengths.

The recent breadth of college and university response to the region's economic needs has been impressive. In each issue area selected for the seminar, there are prime examples of what higher education can do to bolster a region's competitiveness.

Maintaining Technological Leadership
Officials of certain states have created policies, programs,

and agencies to preserve areas of existing technological strength. These policies and agencies create institutionalized relationships among private and public organizations—particularly colleges and universities, firms, business associations, and local governments. The comprehensive packaging of loans, grants, and institutional support extends the reach of limited state resources in an effective way to increase the competitiveness of existing firms and to create better conditions for new enterprise. Important efforts in the Northeast include:

•*State of Pennsylvania Ben Franklin Partnership* (BFP). Growing out of the need to deal with the impact of declining industry sectors, the state in 1982 created this program of public-private partnerships to meet industry needs for new technology. Goals of the BFP are to create jobs and firms in new advanced-technology enterprises and to improve productivity, particularly among existing industries. Central to the mission of the BFP are four Advanced Technology Centers: university-based consortia of universities and colleges, business and industry, organized labor, and economic development groups. Higher education institutions are the centerpiece of the program. In southeastern Pennsylvania, for example, Temple, Drexel, Thomas Jefferson, the University of Pennsylvania, Pennsylvania hospitals, and thirty other public and private universities are involved. Research is supported through the use of challenge grants. In 1986, the state appropriated $29 million and drew $90 million from businesses, foundations, and other sources for research. The state has chosen a decentralized approach to technology development, relying on the initiatives of local groups of research and economic development professionals to define projects for BFP support. Five smaller programs offer technical services and seed capital to small businesses and R&D projects.

•*New York State Science and Technology Foundation*. Through a variety of programs—from small grants to large loans—the foundation uses its nearly $15 million in assets to stimulate research and development, innovation, improved productivity, and capitalization. The programs give high priority to strengthening relationships between a wide range of universities and industry, and to assisting firms throughout the state by improving their access to technology, finance, and marketing information. Among the foundation's programs designed to preserve technological leadership is the Corporation for Innovation Development, which provides start-up capital to new, technology-based ventures. Another such program, the Productivity Development Program, aims to aid the manufacturing sector by awarding matching grants to firms. These funds generally allow the assessment and integration of new, "off-the-shelf" technology to boost productivity. Universities, colleges, and institutes throughout the state cooperate in the program.

• *State of Massachusetts Center of Excellence Program.* Designed to induce sustained growth in regions of the state outside the Route 128 corridor, four centers of excellence have become an important part of the state's economic strategy. This program draws upon the strengths of the participating universities (University of Massachusetts at Amherst, U.-Mass. Medical School in Worcester, Southeastern Massachusetts University, and U.-Mass.-Lowell) and uses the concentration of firms near these universities as a base for further growth. By developing strength in four technology areas (polymers, biotechnology, marine science, and photovoltaics), the university hopes to form industrial clusters for job creation and economic growth. The state government retains a role of coordination: to bring together universities, individual firms and significant organizations; to support centers through annual grants; and to encourage training of students for new firms.

Finance and Service Industries

The importance of services to the nation's economy and future growth is great. Universities and colleges, often supported by state governments, are pursuing new arrangements to produce technological innovations to improve the delivery of services in industries such as finance, telecommunications, computer processing, and medical care. In the Northeast, leading firms are facing greater competition as the ease and speed of communication open more international opportunities for U.S. firms. Examples of university programs to support advanced-service industries in the Northeast include:

• *Polytechnic University Center for Advanced Technology in Telecommunications.* Sponsored by the New York State Science and Technology Foundation, the center brings together the resources of five higher education institutions in New York City (Polytechnic University, and Brooklyn, Medgar Evers, New York City Technical, and Queensborough Colleges). Principal activities include applied research, technical education, and training, with the goal of increasing the participation of the private sector. Research is underway in three different areas: the design of new radio systems, the improvement of image communication, and the application of local area networks to improve office communication. In addition to these programs, three of the participating colleges (Medgar Evers, New York City Technical, and Queensborough Colleges) are developing training programs for the installation and operation of telecommunication equipment. Polytechnic University has designed a postgraduate program in telecommunications management.

• *New England Board of Higher Education Commissions on the New England Economy.* The NEBHE has two distinct, ongoing inquiries into the delivery of legal and medical services. Professionals from industry, higher education, and government have joined the Commission on Academic Health Centers and the New England Economy and the Commission on Legal Education and Practice and the New England Economy. Common themes are how to prepare for continued change in the industries and how to prepare the professions and higher education for increased global competition and technological sophistication. In the health field, the commission will focus on strategies for job creation and new enterprise support, along with other considerations of the emerging biomedical/biotechnology fields. In the legal field, the commission will examine what is apparently a two-tiered legal structure, with large firms and small practices pursuing largely different targets. Other activities of the board include a new study of the internationalization of the New England economy. In addition to detailing the nature of the relationships that states in the region have with foreign countries, the study is examining new priorities for international education.

Traditional Manufacturing in Transition

Universities are continuing to create programs to provide technology transfer and technical assistance for manufacturing sectors striving to adjust to global market conditions. To remain competitive, firms are employing a range of solutions from leading-edge, computer-integrated manufacturing to less sophisticated materials-handling systems. When industrial sectors are structurally outmoded and beyond the reach of technical assistance, universities are deploying resources to help affected workers make the transition to new jobs. Examples of programs in this area range from advanced research to hands-on technical assistance:

• *The George M. Low Center for Industrial Innovation* (CII), Rensselaer Polytechnic Institute (RPI). The center is a focal point for applied research for the manufacturing industries. In 1985, RPI received a matching loan of $30 million from the New York State Science and Technology Foundation to construct the CII for the State Industrial Innovation Extension Service at the university. Providing technical assistance through field representatives with manufacturing and engineering experience, this organization will aim to give firms in the traditional manufacturing sector better access to new technologies. Within the CII, the Center for Manufacturing Productivity and Technology Transfer is a research unit organized to conduct industry-sponsored research in such areas as computer modeling and simulation, CAD/CAM, robot applications, and robot safety.

• *California University of Pennsylvania, Mon Valley Renaissance Program*. Intended to improve the region's response to the changing industrial base of the region, the program offers a comprehensive set of economic development programs for training, small business assistance, and information about federal contracts and grants. Supported jointly by the university and the business sector in the Monongahela Valley, the program is a significant part of the university's commitment to economic development. The university contributes about a third of the total program budget; other sources of funding are corporations, foundations, and state agencies—including the Ben Franklin Program. Among the programs related to manufacturing, the Technology Training Institute provides short-term technical training to local firms. The program for Customized Job Training is designed for workers in firms that have recently purchased a piece of capital equipment or have expanded production facilities. Other programs include the Entrepreneurial Assistance Center, which coordinates services for people interested in starting new businesses in the area.

Distressed Communities

University-based programs are also coping with transitions underway in distressed regions, communities, and neighborhoods of the Northeast. Some of these areas have been severely affected by the loss of large employers because of the closure of plants, or a reliance on a resource-based economy, while others have suffered economic underdevelopment for many years. Assistance to small business is currently an area of particular interest. Examples of programs offering faculty expertise to reduce the failure rate and create jobs are:

• *Boston University School of Management/Urban Business Identification System* (UBI). As part of the Entrepreneurial Management Institute, the school of management has created the program "Managing for Success" to support Boston inner-city residents interested in starting small, neighborhood-based businesses. To complement the program, the Council for Economic Action (CEA), a nonprofit economic development organization, offers the UBI system (developed in conjunction with the First National Bank of Boston). The UBI system identifies small business opportunities with a high probability of success by analyzing an urban area's industrial base and comparing the resulting profile with other U.S. urban areas that have similar demographic, economic, and political characteristics. This information guides interested entrepreneurs to industries with capacity for growth and helps loan officers evaluate the risk of the new venture. Additional support for the program comes from the Massachusetts Venture Capital Corporation, which provides start-up funds. Technical assistance is offered to graduates of the program who succeed in establishing their own business.

• *Marshall University Center for Regional Progress.* Located in southern West Virginia, the center offers technical assistance services to firms suffering from the depressed economic conditions—very low personal income and high unemployment—caused by the decline of coal mining in the region. Since 1984, the center has provided technical assistance, management training, counseling and referral services, and market research to help existing firms create and retain jobs. The center is also dedicated to providing assistance on creating new ventures. This set of activities helps soften West Virginia's reputation for being anti-business, an image that makes recruiting firms to the state difficult. The center maintains a roster of 225 university faculty and staff members who are willing to consult with individuals from the private and public sectors. To reach firms and individuals throughout the state, the center cooperates with the state-funded Center for Education and Research with Industry (also based at Marshall) to tap faculty members at colleges and universities in West Virginia.

Human Resources

As technological innovation changes the nature of production in service and manufacturing industries, firms are seeking assistance from new sources to meet their needs for trained workers. The emerging emphasis in many firms is less on increasing the quantity of new technology and more on improving the capacity of the workers and managers to use new equipment and processes effectively. Colleges, universities, and technical institutes are finding support from government and industry to provide needed expertise. Examples of these new combinations include:

• *Bay State Skills Corporation* (BSSC). Since its inception in 1981, this organization has designed and implemented programs to improve the capacity of the state's labor force. Grants are given to training and education institutions in the state and must be matched by at least equal contributions of money, staff, or equipment from participating companies. Programs span industry needs for training, retraining, and upgrading employees' skills, as well as advanced-level continuing education. BSSC's success results, in part, from the benefits it confers on participating organizations. Firms are able to track information on trends of production and hiring needs, and gain financial incentives to use workers trained through the programs. Colleges, universities, and technical institutes build ties to industry and can leverage the BSSC grants to maintain state-of-the-art facilities to train workers in high-technology fields.

• *Western New York Business Development Consortium*. Affiliated with institutions of higher education in Erie and Niagara Counties, six centers combine to provide training and technical assistance to firms throughout the western region of the state. In the School of Management at the State University of New York at Buffalo (SUNY-Buffalo), the Regional Economic Assistance Center (REAC) is a multidisciplinary unit designed to reach medium-size and large firms. Direct services to governments and businesses include an internship program and the Human Resources Institute. At the Erie Community College, the Small Business Resource Center provides training in human resources management. Other centers are located at the State University of New York College at Buffalo (two center), the Niagara Community College, and the Technology Development Center. Each of the six centers has unique funding and staffing arrangements. The missions of the consortium members are also distinct, with a shared emphasis on avoiding duplication of services and direct competition.

Agenda

Northeast Regional Seminar
April 30-May 1, 1987
Philadelphia, Pennsylvania

Welcoming Address: James McCormick, Chancellor, Pennsylvania State System of Higher Education

Panel Discussion: Perspectives on the Economy of the Northeast and the Roles for Higher Education in Future Economic Development
Moderator: Hoke Smith, President, Towson State University (MD)
Presenters: Charles Bartsch, Director, Economic Development Group, Northeast/Midwest Institute; Elaine Cinelli, Vice President, Council for Economic Action; Edward V. Regan, State Comptroller, State of New York; Jack Corrigan, Regional Director, Economic Development Administration

Seminar Overview: The Higher Education-Economic Development Connection
Introduction: Harold Williams, Executive Secretary, National Association of Management and Technical Assistance Centers; Helen Roberts, Director, Office of Community Development and Public Service, AASCU
Presenter: Tom Chmura, Senior Policy Analyst, Center for Economic Competitiveness, SRI International

Panel Discussion: College and University Initiatives, Addressing Economic Issues in the Northeast
Moderator: Mary Glenzinski, Director of Campus Services, Council of Independent Colleges
Manufacturing in Transition: Homer Pankey, Vice President

for Development and External Relations, California University of Pennsylvania
Finance and Service Industries: John Hoy, Director, New England Board of Higher Education
Distressed Communities: Robert Maddox, Associate Academic Vice President, Marshall University (WV)
Human Resource Development: Ronald Stein, Vice President for Sponsored Programs, State University of New York at Buffalo
Technological Leadership: Philip Singerman, Director, Advanced Technology Center of Southeastern Pennsylvania

Concurrent Workshops: Manufacturing in Transition, Technological Leadership, Finance and Service Industries, Distressed Communities, Human Resource Development

Luncheon Roundtables
Shippensburg University of Pennsylvania Ben Franklin Partnership Program: Anthony Ceddia
SUNY-Buffalo Regional Economic Assistance Center: Gail Parkinson
Marshall University Center for Regional Progress: Robert Maddox
Pennsylvania Technical Assistance Program: Leroy Marlow
The Continental Research Park Development Group: Richard Kahan
ICMA Town Gown Consortium: Geoffrey Bogart
Mansfield University of Pennsylvania Rural Services Institute: Rod Kelchner
AACJC Keeping America Working Program: James McKinney

Concurrent Workshops

Closing Remarks
Summarizer: R. Scott Fosler, Vice President and Director of Government Studies, Committee for Economic Development

Excerpts

James McCormick

A word about the state system in Pennsylvania. In addition to valuing economic revitalization activities and public service, we need to remember that our central mission for many years has been preparing teachers and other professionals society depends on—nurses, teachers, business managers, computer programmers, and so on. We have been preparing human resources, the infrastructure that makes society operate, for a long time. We contribute to the development of all people. We have been concerned with the black and Hispanic population. We've been giving system attention to professional development and such matters. We have been cooperating the last few years with the Ben Franklin partnership: we have twenty projects at twelve of our universities. Money involved in these projects totals $4.8 billion. One of our institutions has $1.5 million in a major initiative in robotics. And so that partnership has been working. We have involved seven members of the business community in the early development of the system as key advisers of the business community—The Business Roundtable. At our fourteen universities, we have fourteen small business centers, continuing partnerships with business and industry. Many of our universities are paying much attention to SRI's guidelines....

Hoke Smith

One of the things corporations look for when they move into an area is the available culture in that area. What museums does it have? What symphonies? What theaters? For all of those, you need audiences. Many of us in academe are involved in the training of those audiences, which support the culture within our regions. By training human resources, we support economic development in that vague category of *climate*—not only the economic climate but also the cultural and social climates. So our institutions play a wide range of roles in economic development. It's useful to keep in mind the breadth of the contribution higher education institutions make to the economic development of their regions....

Charles Bartsch

The economy of the Northeast and the Mid-Atlantic began 1987 in its best shape of the decade. The region's population has stabilized; unemployment has dropped to the lowest in the nation; new businesses and jobs are being created, and the states are in generally healthy fiscal condition. Continued low rates of inflation and low interest rates have fueled a boom in consumer borrowing—the spending that has helped the Northeast tremendously. This trend has been reflected in employment growth in the region's service sector, as well as in finance and retail. Economists predict that New England states will continue to reap jobs from technological growth. A solid recovery is underway in the Mid-Atlantic states as well. New-firm formation rates are high in both areas. There is considerable strength in several elements of the subregional elements of the economy, especially the growth of Boston, Portland (ME), Philadelphia, Baltimore, and other cities as regional service centers for finance, education, information management, and medicine. However, while much of the region has ridden the high-tech and service revolution to an essentially full employment economy, some cities have not participated in the recovery and remain severely distressed. Cities such as Buffalo, Youngstown, and Newark are still having a difficult time making economic adjustments. Great differences exist in the economic futures of cities throughout the region. There are many former one-industry mill or manufacturing towns that were very dependent on a single employer, and they are still facing difficulties. The industrial mix in many of these cities is highly sensitive to labor costs, energy costs, and international competition.

The challenge, therefore, to the Northeast and Mid-Atlantic states is to bring about their participation in economic growth. All the growth need not be high tech.

A key factor in successfully implementing strategies for recovery is the extent and diversity of economic development tools each area has, and these clearly include university resources. We have to pity the places that simply have no private capital to invest or no technical and training talent to tap for their efforts. Because they have no way to replace the lost services or lost industries, they become less attractive sites for new ventures, and these cities face a vicious cycle. Larger cities that retain a substantial manufacturing base should look beyond growth strategies that assist only those industries. The ongoing structural changes in the national economy are characterized by job growth generated by new small businesses. For cities to take advantage of this phenomenon, then, requires their winning of access to the business formation and technology transfer arena.

As universities enter into partnerships with the business community and city government, they also give new entrepreneurs, who are hungry for knowledge and assistance, access to an untapped mine of university resources. This interaction produces even more entrepreneurial activity through synergism within the university faculty. As small companies work more closely with university scientists and other university staff, staff and scientists themselves often branch out and form their own companies, and this attracts even more entrepreneurs.

People with ideas—ranging from faculty members to inventors, from corporate research staff to independent inventors and entrepreneurs—are all beginning to understand that university/city/business partnerships allow access to financing, inexpensive space (through facilities such as incubators), and technical and management assistance (through university resources). They also receive access to highly complex equipment at low cost, to major computer systems, and to other amenities of a university.

Higher education has played an important role in meeting the challenges of economic revitalization of the Northeast and Mid-Atlantic states. As many institutions accept this role, new demands, perhaps a reconfiguration of past practices, are needed. But new opportunities also arise. Clearly it is a win-win situation for both the university and the local government because new businesses bring new jobs and an enhanced tax base, while the university gains opportunities for its faculty to interact with the private sector and to conduct research....

Elaine Cinelli

As you analyze the emergence of high tech, clearly, the role research universities—and most especially MIT—have played cannot be overstated.... The development phase of the high-technology industry in Massachusetts came largely from the growth of existing firms and new start-ups by local entrepreneurs. The development phase is spontaneous, unaided by local interest groups or governments. That's important to know. The Massachusetts government, particularly through activities like the Mass. Technology Development Corporation and the Mass. Industrial Financing Agency, has done a lot to help the industry grow, but initially, most of that growth simply resulted from entrepreneurs who came out of MIT, started small companies, and spun off a whole series of other companies—i.e., unplanned economic development. MIT and, to a lesser extent, Harvard have not seen themselves as key players in economic development. Yet they have been critical to New England's resurgence.

Studies have shown that during the 1960s, over 175 new firms were started by the staff of four research labs and three engineering departments out of MIT alone. I don't think we can talk about this revitalization without understanding that. Kenneth Olson, who started Digital Equipment, came from MIT's Lincoln Lab, and Mr. Wang was at Harvard's computation lab before he started his firm in 1951. MIT has a strong entrepreneurial spirit. The university has consistently encouraged entrepreneurial activity by its faculty.

Tom Chmura

There are many fundamental changes going on in the economy. These changes put new demands on institutions and also provide them with new opportunities.... There's a wide range of possible roles for universities. We often hear about MIT and Stanford and those kinds of special examples, and they're obviously important, but there are a number of important roles smaller institutions can play, too. There are many roles that departments outside of engineering and science can play, that schools of international relations can play, that schools of sociology and social sciences can play. They shouldn't be overlooked. Different kinds of institutions need to respond in different ways. Some institutions have made mistakes when somewhat naively trying to copy some of the more prominent models. The real strength of our American system is its diversity....

But this sort of thing doesn't just happen. As we at SRI looked at institutions around the country, it was clear that good economic development programs are no accident. Some institutions have entrepreneurial leadership and new policies and new faculty incentives and, maybe, some early retirement programs and new organizational arrangements. Those institutions that have been most involved have taken proactive steps to make that involvement happen. It doesn't just naturally evolve in the day-to-day business of a university.... The institutions that have been most successful in economic development are those that have been proactive. They don't sit waiting for industry or state government to give them a grant. They take action and collaborate with other economic development players, and plan strategy in the roles they play for the niches they carve out for themselves in economic development....

Mary Glenzinski:

The Council of Independent Colleges (CIC) project on technological literacy attempts to help undergraduate students understand technology as a model of inquiry and an action-oriented, interactive, problem-solving process that emphasizes such critical skills as quantitative reasoning, decision making, and the understanding of systems. The ultimate goal of the project is to see the technological mode of inquiry accepted in the liberal arts curriculum as equal to the more traditional methods of the sciences and the humanities. We want to help liberal arts students build an ingrained understanding of the scientist's and the engineer's techniques and tools of inquiry. This requires that educators rethink and refocus the traditional liberal arts curriculum to include the study of technology. As important as this is now, it will become imperative as technology becomes an increasingly powerful force in society and our economy more and more knowledge based....

The two curricular modules involving successful campus-corporate partnerships that I would like to detail are called "The City" and "The Natural Environment." "The City" is conceived and taught at Emmanuel College, a women's college of about 1,100 students in Boston. It is a course about Boston and its transportation systems. The course has as its broad objective the teaching of a range of knowledge required to carry on a major engineering project and to understand the interdependence of society and technology. After an overview of the history and current patterns of urbanization worldwide is presented by the course and structures, some of you may find this a marvelous partnership—a sociologist and a historian. The students form research teams and go out into the city to investigate how decisions are made, jobs scheduled, funding required, and technical problems solved by looking at Boston's transportation system—specifically, Boston's Red Line extension, the Southwest corridor, and planning stages of the underground's central artery and Third Harbor Tunnel....

Ultimately, the students are to understand the historical, economic, political, and social dimensions of urban transportation systems by analyzing the impact of such change on actual neighborhoods and learning how civil authorities, engineers, and construction workers work together toward progress. The course is complemented by a year-long lecture series, this year entitled "Technology and the Transformation of Urban Life." The lectures are open to faculty, students, and the public, and cover such topics as transportation and the future of Boston, and the impact of fourteen million square feet of commercial space on Boston life....

During the fall of 1986, Alaska Pacific University, a private college in Anchorage with an enrollment of 782 students, placed emphasis on technological literacy through its sophomore core course, "The Natural Environment," one of eight core courses devoted to promoting scientific and technological literacy. Alaska Pacific structured the natural environment course around the theme of telecommunications, chosen because of its tremendous impact on Alaska, especially during the last decade. Using telecommunications as a focal point of the course, they presented immediate problems—foremost among them, Alaska Pacific's small faculty, having marginal expertise in the area of communications. Certainly it would have been easier to choose another theme, but the relevance of the topic seemed to outweigh the risks of venturing into areas where expertise was not available on campus. To mitigate this problem, Alaska Pacific joined forces with Alascom Incorporated, a company of approximately 1,000 employees considered synonymous with modern telecommunications in Alaska. During the last fifteen years, Alascom has built a system that implements many conveniences—same-day news coverage, direct long-distance dialing, live sporting events, etc.—that the lower forty-eight states take for granted.

Through the expertise of Alascom, students received a comprehensive picture of recent advances in telecommunications. One set of lectures, which illustrated how Alaska Pacific and Alascom cooperated, dealt with satellite communications. Students had several assigned readings for a general introduction to the topic. During one class period, students constructed an FM receiver, taking a bag of a few electronic components and building an antenna out of wire, a power system from batteries, and a tuner from a capacitor. It was felt students could better appreciate and understand the systems needed to deliver long-distance communication via satellite. The exercise was taught by an Alaska Pacific faculty member.

After the readings and lab activity, a senior employee from Alascom, who was at one time chief of the Alascom Satellite Division, gave a presentation on modern satellite telecommunications. This guest lecturer touched on many issues mentioned in the readings and answered questions that were beyond the expertise of the regular instructor. The module of lessons concluded with a field trip to one of Alascom's Gateway Earth satellites to view the tools that make satellite communication possible....

These problems show that the basic concepts of technology and the technological mode of problem solving can be taught in any field, not just in transportation or in communications. Technological literacy, quantitative skills, decision making and analysis, and other applied processes are the tools of the technologist but are also tools with which any liberally educated person should be familiar. In this project...students are helped to understand that high technology is much more than machines, scientific experiments, or computerized bank statements: it is a concept that is changing the way they live, the way they learn, and the way they function and make judgments in an information and knowledge-based society....

Homer Pankey

In 1983, our president, Dr. John Curtis Watkins, realized that California University of Pennsylvania had to do something to help reverse declining economic trends in southwestern Pennsylvania.... The majority of its steel plants, at least in the Pittsburgh area, are gone; they are being bulldozed and blasted out of existence, and the land is being turned into industrial parks or waterfront property. But the workers remain. So our president had the foresight to say that California University of Pennsylvania had a public-service obligation to help these people and their businesses.

We set up a program that had three elements: first, to aid the existing business and industries to improve, stabilize, or expand. It's a classic example in that 80 percent of business growth within a region has to come from the existing economic base.... Second, we targeted new businesses that were arriving in the area, though not at the level of effort we put toward the existing businesses. The labor climate during those years was viewed negatively by outside people, and it was hard to attract new businesses. Third, we attempted to stimulate entrepreneurs to start their own businesses....

We put together the entrepreneur's assistance center, a program that works with businesses to help people acquire bank loans and do business planning, product analysis, and site location. We had a tremendous amount of help from the major utility companies—West Penn Power Company, People's Natural Gas Company, Duquesne Power, Equitable Gas. These companies were very much involved because they, like California University of Pennsylvania, cannot pull up their power lines and gas lines and move elsewhere, and we are not going to move our campus. So we have to improve the area in which we live....

We do not simply sit down with entrepreneurs and help them formulate a business plan: we actually help them type it. We help them prepare their loan applications. We take them to venture capitalists. We go with them to the bank to help make their presentations. It's a hand-holding job all the way....

We also run a government agency coordination office. We have helped businesses and individuals obtain $4.5 million worth of financing—either conventional financing, SBA financing, PITA, or venture capital money. The coordination office helps businesses in the area compete for and win government contracts.... To do this, we have set up a contracting office, staffed with skilled people, and we help entrepreneurs prepare bids. We do everything except calculating their dollar value for the product. Our computers can give a bid history of the past three years on nuts and bolts or airplane parts or whatever the contract calls for, so our clients know whether their bid will be competitive. We then go with them to the plants and do an on-site inspection prior to the government's inspection.... In the last year we helped 160 firms successfully bid on and win $7.5 million of new government business....

John Hoy

I have been asked to focus on finance and services and the role of higher education in economic development of this sector.... The first fundamental change I think we have to understand is the shift from an industrial to an information economy in which more than 60 percent of America's work force are employed in the creation, organization, and distribution of information—people such as programmers, teachers, clerks, lawyers, consultants, secretaries, accountants, writers, stock brokers, managers, insurers, civil servants, architects, bankers, and to a large extent, technicians. Today, the goods-producing sector accounts for only 33 percent of the GNP of the United States. New England, with 260 colleges, is tied to a highly concentrated and elaborate network of scientific and technological research centers that serve not a technological economy, but a knowledge-intensive economy, for which service is a large component. The strategic economic resource of the future has become knowledge, brain power, and information....

Our largest service sector is the 512,000 people who work in health care. The second-largest is the education community of the New England region, employing well over 450,000 people. New England's piece of the high-technology world of this nation represents 233,000 jobs, and we are delighted about that. But the services sector is much more vast....

In the area of services and finance for New England, the new infrastructure of this small economy, tucked into the northeastern corner of the country, is basically its R&D capacity. With 5 percent of the U.S. population, the New England region pulls down 12 percent of all federal research dollars granted to colleges and universities in the country. It pulls down about 18 percent of all grants associated with the National Institutes of Health and the biomedical complex, in particular. In areas such as the environment, federal grants to New England exceed the 20-percent level, and astonishingly, in terms of grants to the New England region and its colleges, universities, and non-profit institutes, this tiny part of the world pulls down 40.6 percent of all Department of Defense R&D grants in the United States. With that concentration of intellectual and knowledge-based activity, one would have to ask, "What is this? A service economy or a military industrial complex?" Basically, it's neither. It's a sort of emergent information economy. While the Northeast has prided itself essentially on the skill and the imagination and the level of formal education its population has attained, one of the most disturbing trends is our persistence in essentially planning to waste 30 percent of the young people of our region who do not graduate from high school and who today are relegated to a position in the economic pecking order and that segment of what we call the "Taco Bell service economy" out of which it will become increasingly difficult for them to emerge at a later date....

Robert Maddox

The Center for Regional Progress was literally a bridge. We were awarded a grant from the Economic Development Administration to establish a university center program. The Administration was concerned about job creation, new investments, retention of jobs, technical research assistance, feasibility studies, government policy plans, and so forth. When we established our university center program as part of the Center for Regional Progress, we did so by using a good portion of the grant money to allow the problems that come to us to be solved by faculty members here, whatever their expertise. In some cases, it might be three professors from the business school. In other cases, it might be an interdisciplinary team from the colleges of liberal arts, science, and education....

We have added a Small Business Development Center as part of the statewide network. It, too, is part of the Center for Regional Progress, and this structure ensures that what the Small Business Development Center does for entrepreneurs and small business owners complements, without duplicating, what our EDA program does....

We also have been asked to operate for our board of regents a Regents Center for Education and Research with Industry (CERI), which is a statewide network. We recently had an outside consultant examine the CERI network, and he was pleased to see that it was working—that we were actually getting, one, two, and in some cases, three institutions cooperating to help solve a problem in a given part of the State of West Virginia....

We have also established by state law an Institute for International Trade Development. It started out 2-1/2 years ago as a global trade conference made possible by our EDA funds. This activity led to an export director on the State of West Virginia and then to a major study for the state legislature and the establishment of that office. We have statewide responsibility for that service, which we deliver through our CERI network....

Ron Stein

I would like to provide a brief glimpse of different roles the University of New York at Buffalo plays in support of regional economic development, and I would argue that these roles can be played by any university in any region of the country. The first role is that of economic development leader. The second is that of the university's own economic activities, and the third is of support system for other economic development activities.

SUNY-Buffalo is the leading and most comprehensive public research university in New York State, with over 27,000 students, including 8,000 graduate and professional students and 11,000 employees, and receives a quarter of a billion dollars a year in direct state support. If we view the university as a large corporation, it is fair to say that New York State and its taxpayers are the university's shareholders. As such, we feel we have a special obligation to respond to their problems. It should not be a surprise that one of the major problems facing New York State, particularly western New York, is economic development. The president of the university believes, in view of the public-service mission of the university, that one of his primary responsibilities is to serve as one of the economic development leaders of New York State and western New York. In this capacity, he has spoken to hundreds of community, political, and business groups on the economic future of western New York and what needs to be done. He serves as a member of a small group of Buffalo business executives whose sole agenda is the development of programs to bring about the revitalization of the economy of western New York. He chairs the Western New

York Regional Economic Council, a gubernatorial-appointed group of business, political, and labor leaders, charged to develop a strategic plan for economic revitalization of the eight western New York counties and to present proposals to the governor's office for funding from the state's $20-million regional economic development (RED) fund. To date this group has successfully competed for over $3 million of these RED funds. The president has, in every address in the university community, emphasized the university's role in supporting the economic development of the region. By setting this as one of his highest priorities, he has encouraged the faculty and staff to aggressively seek opportunities to help the business community of our region.

The university's own efforts in economic development directly have been substantial. The university successfully competed for the National Center for Earthquake Engineering Research. This initial grant of $25 million for five years from the National Science Foundation was matched in the first year by $5 million of New York State funds. The state match was based on the clear belief that there was substantial economic development opportunity in having this National Center at Buffalo. The university has successfully obtained a $3-million grant to build a new high-tech incubator adjacent to its North Campus. The old incubator, which exists near its South Campus in buildings built during the Erie Canal days but is only less than three years old as an incubator, is already fully occupied with seventeen firms. The new incubator will provide entrepreneurs with flexible wet-lab space at below-market rates to enhance their efforts to grow new companies. Other support will be in the form of computer marketing and financial assistance. After a 2-3-year period, a decision will be made either to graduate these companies from the incubator into other spaces in western New York, thereby seeding economic rebirth of the region, or phase out the activity.

The university recently developed a Center for Industrial Effectiveness, to help manufacturers pinpoint their problems and, when public funds are available, how to use them most effectively. The short-term objectives will be to stabilize and modernize western New York's existing industries in an effort to preserve high-wage, skilled jobs in a heavy industrial base. Concentration will be on industries that may be feasibly restructured to meet the demands of national and international markets. The center aims to assemble technical insights for aging industries by tapping into the resources of the economic institutions throughout the area and any other outside sources of expertise. We will recruit and screen prospective companies and then study their operations, including such areas as material handling, energy efficiency, quality control, and even marketing, accounting, and industrial relations....

Philip Singerman

Pennsylvania is not traditionally known as a state that has innovative economic development programs in high technology. It is a traditional manufacturing state that has, over the last couple of decades, suffered many of the problems of all of the northeastern manufacturing states. Established in 1983, the Ben Franklin Program is a relatively new program that has given the state a national reputation among state programs and, within the state, is identified as the most successful economic program by both parties of the legislature and the two governors of different political parties.

The program started in 1983 with $1 million for the challenge grant program; this year it has $28 million. Cumulatively, the legislature has appropriated $75 million to date for the Ben Franklin Partnership. In addition, as a result of the success of the base program, other programs have been put into place; a $4.5-million venture fund, $3 million for engineering equipment, $1.5 million for seed investments directly to small companies, and half a dozen other programs, none of which existed four years ago....

Our advanced technology program defines advanced technology very broadly as not only the development of new technologies but the application of existing ones. It is managed by a state program, the Ben Franklin Partnership. The program is decentralized, run by four technology centers throughout

Pennsylvania, each of which is located at a university or university consortium, and indeed, each of the centers is now or will be soon operated under an independent nonprofit corporation.... We fund activities in research and development, education and training, and business assistance, and I think that's crucial to the development of a successful and broad political base for any program. We operate on a consortial basis involving business, universities, government, and—I would point out as important—labor, often a neglected constituent in economic development programs.... Our program is managed by the University City Science Center, a nonprofit corporation owned by twenty-eight colleges, universities, and health institutions in the Delaware Valley. Within the Science Center, the Advanced Technology Center is autonomous. We have our own board, and our program is administered and managed by a series of technology advisory councils or peer review committees. Funding decisions are made on the basis of the technical merits of proposals and are made by knowledgeable and committed committees....

We have a successful project called the Small Business Innovation Office, which helps companies apply for federal small business innovation research (SBIR) contracts (half a billion dollars set aside for small R&D companies).... Pennsylvania is the fourth or fifth largest recipient of SBIR grants, though you would not predict that outcome from the state's demographics or history. It is a consequence of program activity sponsored by universities and the state. Every state can do that; every university can do that. It's a market niche that's not being filled currently by other sectors and has a tremendous payoff for companies....

Higher Education,
Economic Development,
and the West

Overview

The United States has entered a new era of global competition and falling world commodities prices. The western region of the United States has been hard hit because of its traditional reliance on natural-resource-based commodities industries such as agriculture, forest products, mineral extraction, and energy and the new vulnerabilities of its technology-based industries such as electronics, computers, and aerospace.

The traditional competitive advantages enjoyed by the region—including abundant natural resources, strategic location, and technological leadership—have in many cases been either counterbalanced or superseded by those of other nations. A region that in the 1970s performed better economically than the nation as a whole has, in the 1980s, done worse.

Historically, colleges and universities have played critical roles in the region's economic development. But the region now faces a new set of competitive challenges that require new kinds of responses from higher education. These challenges include:

•*Dual Urban/Rural Economics*. In nearly every western state, a widening gap has been developing between two economies: a largely rural one, based on natural resource industries, and a largely urban one, based on technology and service industries (such as computers, electronics, aerospace, tourism, and financial services).

•*International Trade*. In 1982, for the first time ever, the volume of trade crossing the Pacific exceeded that which crossed the Atlantic, but by 1986 California's trade deficit also topped $20 billion, and other western states were clearly falling behind.

•*Technological Development and Transfer*. Competitors are commercializing more and more of the region's basic and applied research and then using high-quality/low-cost manufacturing processes to gain leadership in emerging markets.

•*New and Small Business Development*. Support in technology application, international marketing, and management education is needed to help new and smaller firms meet competitive challenges from abroad and help them capitalize on opportunities in growing international markets.

• *Human Resource Development.* To address all the preceding concerns, the region must have a skilled and adaptable work force, from top managers to first-line technicians. This requires new, flexible education and training approaches, from community colleges to flagship universities.

Many colleges and universities in the region are making a special effort to help industry adapt and to prepare their students for new economic realities. The western regional seminar reviewed these efforts and explored what more could be done to help the region.

Historical Roles of Higher Education in the Economy of the West

Historically, colleges and universities in the West have played important roles in the continuing adaptation of the region's economy and have been linked in a number of ways to the region's major industries.

Up until World War II, many of the region's most prestigious institutions built their reputations as sources of agricultural or mining and education and research. Some, such as the Colorado School of Mines, actually concentrated on supporting the human resource and research needs of a single industry. Others, such as the University of Nebraska or University of California-Davis, developed critical roles in agriculture.

During the World War II era, many institutions began assuming leadership in other disciplines as well. In California, for example, University of California-Berkeley established its radiation laboratory and contributed significantly to the development of the atomic bomb, established Berkeley as a center for research in nuclear physics, and attracted much federal research support for nuclear labs in Livermore and Los Alamos. Similarly, the California Institute of Technology became famous for its contributions to astronomy, physics, and rocketry and was thus a key supporter in the development of the West Coast's aerospace industry.

After World War II, many colleges in the region expanded their activities to address the needs of immigrants from the Midwest and East. And they expanded their research base to accommodate a more diversified economy. Substantial defense spending spawned a great deal of scientific research in the region, especially in California, Washington, Colorado, and New Mexico. Institutions such as UCLA and the University of Minnesota developed leadership positions in engineering that helped serve the needs of southern California's burgeoning defense industry and Minnesota's computer industry respectively.

Private institutions also developed important roles during the postwar period. The University of Southern California excelled in petroleum geology and served the needs of the West Coast's growing petroleum industry. Meanwhile, under the leadership of Dr. Fred Terman, Stanford's excellence in engineering helped attract top faculty and student talent, and its progressive attitude toward industrial collaboration led to the development of the nation's first major university-related industrial park and helped support the development of California's high-technology industry in Silicon Valley.

However, while the contributions of private institutions have been significant, public higher education has been more important to the West than to almost any other region of the country. Because of the relative lack of strong private institutions in the West and because of its widely dispersed population, state governments needed to take the lead in providing access to higher education and research for distant and sparsely populated areas.

While the contribution of the region's leading research universities has clearly been important, the role of state colleges and universities and community colleges has been particularly valuable in the West. Many institutions have evolved from teachers colleges into comprehensive state universities actively involved in their region's economy. San Jose State University, for example, not Stanford or Berkeley, is the leading producer of engineers for Silicon Valley. And institutions such as California

Polytechnic State University San Luis Obispo have developed important agricultural and technical strengths that have enabled them to become major contributors to their local and regional economies.

The West also has over 240 community and technical colleges that together serve more than 1.5 million students and account for more than half of the region's postsecondary enrollment. The expansion of these public systems after World War II has been critical to the development of the region's economy and the education and training of one of the highest skilled work forces in the nation. For example, institutions such as Foothill and De Anza Colleges in Silicon Valley and Maricopa Colleges in Arizona are critical sources of technical training for high-technology firms.

Higher Education Responses to the Economic Challenges of the West

An array of innovative linkages to economic development has appeared among the region's colleges and universities. These steps are clearly important in helping the region's economy adapt to new global economic realities. They are, in many cases, pilot initiatives—the first attempt to come to grips with an entirely new competitive environment. To enhance regional competitiveness, these initiatives must be replicated, expanded, or otherwise institutionalized. Other initiatives will no doubt also need to be adopted. But it is not clear what the next step should be. The western regional seminar provided a forum for discussing the next steps, and for determining the appropriate role of higher education in helping the region meet its economic challenges.

Human Resource Development

The new global economy requires a broader understanding of other cultures, an ability to react quickly to market changes, and a capacity to learn new technologies. In short, industry needs a skilled and adaptable work force. In response to recent trends, colleges and universities in the region have begun to adapt current programs and introduce new initiatives with this aim in mind:

•*Arizona State University Engineering Excellence Program.* As Arizona has become home to a growing number of high-technology firms, a work force with new, higher levels of technical skills has come into demand. As some of these companies began to leave the state in search of adequately skilled labor, Arizona State reached out to local industry and together assembled a comprehensive five-year plan to bolster education and research in several areas critical to the state's emerging technological economy. The university is currently implementing a second five-year development plan that will add a new specialization in telecommunications and tap the expertise of other departments (e.g., business and humanities) in support of economic development objectives.

•*California Community College industry training consortia.* Community colleges have also begun to explore new approaches to helping their regions adapt to economic change. The industry training consortium is one model that has become increasingly popular in California. In the San Francisco Bay area, a nationally recognized Telecommunications Training Consortium of local companies worked with the San Mateo County Community College District to design new curricula and develop a fully equipped telecommunications laboratory. Similarly, a consortium of aerospace companies has developed a relationship with a network of community colleges in southern California. A community college/industry linkages task force has been organized by the Bay Area Council (a business policy group) to promote further collaboration of this type in the Bay area.

•*University of California-Los Angeles CAD/CAM Project.* Concerned that new engineering graduates were not keeping up with fast-moving CAD/CAM technology, several southern California aerospace firms worked with UCLA to donate up-to-date hardware and software, organize seminars, establish fellowships, endow a faculty chair, and undertake joint research projects. The focus is multidisciplinary, tapping the university's engineering, applied science, and computer science departments in a concerted effort to better meet changing human resource requirements.

International Relations and Trade

Recently, much attention has been focused on the need to understand foreign cultures, languages, and markets in order to compete successfully in the new global economy. For example, a recent California State University commission focused on the specific challenges and opportunities presented by the growing Pacific Rim region. In response to international trade concerns, colleges and universities in states throughout the region have taken action:

• *University of Washington Center for International Trade in Forest Products*. Established in 1984, the center conducts research and develops strategies to expand the state's international trade in basic and manufactured forest products. The center monitors foreign markets, assesses the status of the state's forest product industries, and coordinates, develops, and disseminates technical and market information to local industry. Located within the college of forest resources, the center has established linkages with the schools of law, business, and international studies; the State of Washington and the USDA Forest Service; and major Washington forest product manufacturers.

• *University of California-San Diego Graduate School of International Relations and Pacific Studies*. Established in 1986, the school is the only professional school of international relations in the University of California system. The school will offer two degree programs: a professional master's program in Pacific International Affairs and a research-oriented Ph.D. program. Midcareer and other intensive short programs will be developed as well. The school will also seek to be a center of research excellence on economic, social, political, technological, and other issues confronting Pacific Rim nations. Training and research in both the private and public policy domains are anticipated.

•*California State University-San Francisco internationalization of business curriculum.* Previously, only international business majors (5 percent of total business majors) were exposed to significant international business concepts and practices. Today, a great number of courses contain a large international segment, a practice that now affects virtually all business students. A variable topics course provides insights into many different cultures, and opportunities now exist for work-study in cooperation with the U.S.-Japan Institute, the Center for World Business, and the U.S.-China Institute.

• *University of Idaho International Trade and Development Office.* The office was established to facilitate and oversee international programs and activities at the university. It works with university faculty and industry representatives to develop teaching, research, and related assistance helpful to making Idaho products more competitive in world markets. The office also serves as an information and networking center, sponsoring an array of special courses, lectures, and conferences, and interacting with a variety of organizations and individuals.

New and Small Business Development

It has been well documented that in the past decade the majority of new jobs have been created by small and medium-size businesses. It is also true that the failure rate among these firms is quite high. Clearly, it is in the region's best interest to see that its small businesses receive the assistance they need to prosper, be it financial, managerial or technological. Pilot efforts at several colleges and universities have begun to address this need:

• *California Institute of Technology RIMTech program.* The Research Institute for the Management of Technology (RIMTech) was founded in 1986 with funds from NASA, the state department of commerce, and a consortium of small high-technology companies. The program matches executives—mostly from smaller firms that cannot afford a sophisticated R&D facility—with engineers and others at the Jet Propulsion Laboratory in Pasadena to explore technology transfer opportunities. Typi-

cally, companies communicate their top research needs to JPL engineers, who in turn brainstorm with company officials about ways to utilize appropriate technologies to address these needs.
• *University of Colorado-Boulder Small Business Assistance Center.* The special emphasis of the center is on small businesses located in rural areas of Colorado. The center provides one-on-one consulting in financing, market research, and business planning, as well as seminars and referral services. Center professionals possess not only various general business expertise, but also substantive knowledge of specific industries important to the Colorado economy, such as oil and gas, tourism, data processing, retailing, and manufacturing. Branch offices provide services to remote areas of the state.
• *University of Hawaii Pacific Business Center Program.* This program is sponsored by the university and the U.S. Department of Commerce. It operates through faculty associates (as well as graduate student associates) in a variety of disciplines who are on call to help solve specific problems affecting small business growth and blocking expansion into new markets. Specific projects include technical or managerial assistance to develop a new business or a new product or service for an existing small business.

Technology Development and Transfer
The region's higher education system has always played a key role in technological development, either through pioneering research or education of future entrepreneurs. However, because of increasing competitive pressure from other nations, the region must develop and apply new technologies faster than ever before. Programs such as those listed below are indicative of higher education's most recent efforts to keep the West on the leading edge of technology development and application:
• *UCLA/USC Institute for Manufacturing Automation Research.* The University of California-Los Angeles and the University of Southern California, in collaboration with a consortium of private firms, are establishing a manufacturing research center. The new Institute for Manufacturing Automation Research will

provide a vehicle for joint industry-university activities to rejuvenate the state's manufacturing sector. University faculty will direct and industry representatives will supervise applied research essential to manufacturing competitiveness. The institute will also serve as a centralized training facility to prepare production engineers for industry.

• *California State University-Sacramento Applied Research and Design Center.* The center is used as a vehicle to organize collaborative efforts between university scientists and engineers and those in industry. It draws on a pool of nearly 100 faculty to work on tailored projects that improve the basic operations of local industry. Hewlett-Packard and Intel have helped the university's engineering school design a new computer curriculum and establish an extension learning center to help industry adapt to new skill demands.

• *Science and Technology Resource Center at Southwest State University* (MN). This center was established in 1985 by the Minnesota state legislature as a "pilot project for regional economic development." The purpose of the center is to encourage and assist inventors, entrepreneurs, and small businesses to develop new products and processes for the continued economic development of southwestern Minnesota. Projects developed through the center include the development of new crops and food-processing and manufacturing facilities and equipment.

Regional Economic Development—Urban and Rural

Both urban and rural colleges and universities in the West have begun to respond to the needs of their communities in new ways. In some cases, this has meant helping urban governments address difficult growth issues or assisting rural governments to pursue economic diversification. Prime examples of this kind of community capacity-building by higher education include:

• *University of Colorado-Denver Center for the Improvement of Public Management and Center for Public-Private Sector Cooperation.* Two special centers within the university's school of public affairs have become the foci for capacity-building assistance to groups in Colorado and the Rocky Mountain region.

The Center for the Improvement of Public Management trains managers to tackle such challenges as political leadership and conflict resolution in economic development and strategic planning. The Center for Public-Private Sector Cooperation brings together diverse parties to address community issues such as economic development. Expertise in strategic planning, program management, media relations, and public participation is applied to generate innovative, collaborative approaches to community problems.

•*Eastern Oregon State College Regional Services Institute.* Some rural institutions have sought to improve their region's capacity to attract and sustain new economic development. Eastern Oregon State's Regional Services Institute is an example. The institute responds to the needs of local rural governments for technical expertise in many areas relating to economic development. Institute staff assist in the planning of infrastructure, the assembling of marketing packages to attract industry, the conducting of surveys and special studies, the writing of grants, and other activities.

•*Washington State University IMPACT Center.* In an effort to assist hard-hit rural farming areas, the State Department of Agriculture joined with Washington State University to form the IMPACT Center. The goal of the program is to expand the university's research effort in international agricultural marketing, and to identify and develop alternative uses for farmland in eastern Washington.

•*University Center for Economic Development and Planning at California State University, Chico.* The purpose of this EDA-supported center is to improve the capacity of public and private entities in northern California to plan and carry out effective economic development efforts. The center, through research, information dissemination, technical assistance, and training and referral services, uses the university's organizational structure to assist the public and private sectors in combatting economic distress in this area of California.

Agenda

Western Regional Seminar
February 4-5, 1988
Palo Alto, CA

Welcome
Steven Waldhorn, Director, Center for Economic Competitiveness, SRI International; Chia-Wei Woo, President, San Francisco State University

Opening Address
Theodore Sanger, President and CEO (Retired), Pacific Bell, and Chairman, California Economic Development Corporation

Panel Discussion—Perspectives on the Economy
Chair: William Miller, President, SRI International
Presenters: Bryan Murphy, Staff Director, Joint Legislative Committee for the Master Plan, California Legislature; Patricia Hill Hubbard, Vice President for Education and Science Policy, American Electronics Association and Member, California Community College Board of Trustees; David Longanecker, Executive Director of the Minnesota Higher Education Coordinating Board

Luncheon Address
Larry Blake, President, Oregon Institute of Technology

Panel Discussion—College and University Initiatives
Chair: Radford King, Executive Director, Western Research Applications Center, University of Southern California
Presenters: Steven Altman, President ,Texas A&I University (Human Resources); Warren Baker, President, California Polytechnic State University, San Luis Obispo (Technical Transfer); Donald Gerth, President, Sacramento State University (International Trade); Patty Martillaro, Director, Small Business

Assistance Center, University of Colorado at Boulder (Small Business Development); Leon Boothe, President, Northern Kentucky University (Urban Economic Development); Ruth Leventhal, Provost/Dean, Pennsylvania State University at Harrisburg (Rural/Community Development)

Concurrent Workshops
Human Resources—Ellis McCune, President, California State University, Hayward
International Trade—Harold Haak, President, California State University, Fresno
Technical Transfer—Radford King, Executive Director, Western Research Applications Center, University of Southern California
Small Business—Jude Valdez, Director, Center for Economic Development, University of Texas at San Antonio
Urban Economic Development—Thomas Stauffer, President, University of Houston-Clear Lake
Rural/Community Development—David Gilbert, President, Eastern Oregon State College

Remarks by Cosponsoring Organizations
Tom Chmura, Program Manager, SRI International
J. Carter Rowland, Consultant to Office of Academic Programs, AASCU
Mary Gordon, Program Associate, Office of Academic Programs, AASCU

Dinner Address
Aims McGuiness, Associate Executive Director for Higher Education, Education Commission of the States

State University Networks
Robert Carothers, Chancellor, Minnesota State University System
Ralph Alterowitz, IBM Executive Consultant on Loan to AASCU

Closing Remarks
John Woodward, Regional Director, EDA, Seattle

Excerpts

Chia-Wei Woo

The thesis of liberal arts education is at once noble and functional. It calls for a breadth of knowledge and an in-depth appreciation of disciplines. It offers students the power to seek and determine values. It enables students to learn how to learn. The concept is positive and proactive. Somehow, through the voice of some of its current defenders, the concept has taken on a stridently antiprofessional tone. The expressed desire on the part of students to use college education to launch personal careers, and thereby participate in the economic development of society, is depicted as antithetical to a sound liberal arts education. I, for one, have always thought of a liberal arts education as one that strengthens and enriches professionalism, rather than one that excludes and confronts. It is thus disheartening to see self-styled proponents of the liberal arts education define the latter narrowly in classical terms or from shallow experiences that predated the advent of postwar technology. I cringe when I hear colleagues who have never had a meaningful laboratory course or have never appreciated the beauty of logic in mathematics, lambast what they *perceive* as computer science. While taking pride in not having ever been seen in the vicinity of a computer terminal, such a person may, nonetheless, be totally dependent on a manual typewriter, forgetting that the latter is a technological dinosaur. Can you think of any attitude more unliberal than that?

It is perhaps not surprising, then, that the champions of economic development—i.e., the leaders of industry, business, and labor— feel alienated by the more self-righteous faction of our college faculty. University administrators, who invariably come from faculty ranks, find themselves caught between what is thought of as liberal arts on one side and professional education on the other. They carry an innate fear of betraying the "liberal arts" tradition and ideal. That they have generally failed to adopt effective measures in promoting economic development in their regions is clearly not accidental....

Our school of science operates a center for environmental studies on the shores of Tiburon in Marin County. On the thirty-acre site, there is much academic research carried out on marine biology, water conservation, and estuarian sciences, all sponsored by federal and state agencies. In recent years, we have gone into aquaculture and genetic studies, as well, in collaboration with start-up companies. We have also established a Bay Conference Center to facilitate dialogues and foster cooperation among education, business, and the community.

Our school of creative arts sees the emergence of high technology as an opportunity for the arts, one that renders new tools and new dimensions. In return, industry needs to acquire user input on applications and vision. Technological development is no longer a matter of manufacturers providing and customers ordering finished products, but one of collaboration on both conceptualization and design. Applications software and CAD/CAM are obvious examples. Future cooperative projects will have the use of a new on-campus $15-million arts-and-industry facility to be funded by the state— in recognition of the new frontiers shared by arts and industry.

Our school of business has always been at the forefront of meeting regional needs and has provided services to business in the form of consultation and conferences through centers that focus on small businesses and world trade. On the latter, the school operates U.S.-Japan, U.S.-Korea, U.S.-Canada, and U.S.-China Business institutes and engages in active cooperation with the Commonwealth Club, World Affairs Council, World Trade Center, and many of the sixty-five consulates in San Francisco. Recently, it has taken a leading role in setting up the university's joint enterprise with NASA's Ames Research Center. The San Francisco State University Foundation now manages a 126-university consortium in a tripartite effort that engages the private sector in developing NASA's R&S results into prototype products and eventually marketable goods.

Patricia Hill Hubbard

The yesteryear formula wherein a university researcher spun a creative idea out from the university into a local start-up firm no longer seems to be the only path for transfer of technology. Why has this changed? Is it because the faculty itself has changed—that young researchers, often foreign-born, may prefer the academic environment to high-risk start-ups? Is this compounded by the overall aging and less financially risk-oriented faculty? What are other mechanisms for moving basic research ideas out of the university and into the product development phase? Has academe come to view tech transfer and commercialization differently? Is tech transfer, as a recent report described it, a "body contact sport"—occurring when academicians and industrial people get to know one another "up close"? If so, what are academic researchers doing to promote this serious play? The American Electronics Association's view is that tech transfer takes place only when both industry and education identify a community of interest....

Two last issues affecting tomorrow's work force, more controversial than the others mentioned, relate to higher education's role in preparing women and minorities for high-tech careers and improving continuing technical education for today's workers. Over the last decade, electronics companies have struggled to comply with federal EEO regulations, undertaking costly recruiting and in-plant training of women and minorities. The federal regulatory view has been that industry hiring should reflect a percentage of the available women and minorities in a given job category nationwide. However, when one talks about 3 percent of the female population nationally having engineering degrees, it takes a monumental effort to uncover this percentage no matter how good one's recruiting is. The federal view ignored the fact that the educational pipeline has trickled forth too few women or minorities educated for high-tech jobs.

Federal compliance will increasingly be replaced by industry's self-interest over the next 10-20 years as women and minorities become the major source of new employees. Is it not then worth considering that all segments of education come under some sort of formal affirmative action requirement? This idea goes beyond present Title IX relating to hiring of faculty and administrators. Such affirmative action accountability would require aggressive outreach by all of education to recruit and retain women and minority students in nontraditional subjects. Goals would be, for example, to have X-number of women enroll and successfully complete first-year algebra; X-number of minorities enroll and complete Physics 1A, etc. Does this country have time to continue to rely on present voluntary methods that have made some improvement but not to the degree necessary?

Last, 80 percent of today's workers will be working past the turn of the next century. The rate of technological change has accelerated dramatically and will continue to do so. Superconductivity, for example, has the capacity to change almost every aspect of our personal and professional lives. All workers must have skill flexibility—i.e., adaptability. It is far from clear, however, whose primary responsibility it is to deliver continuing technical education— education's or industry's? Most community colleges consider continuing technical education to be one of their two missions and perform the task well— although this is not always as fully appreciated as it should be at the state level....

David Longanecker

There is a danger that we will come to believe that the link between education and economic development is a new discovery. It is not. Enhancing the economic vitality of our states always has been at least one of our principal reasons for investing public funds in postsecondary education. Why is it dangerous to claim economic development as a novel idea, even if it is not? It is dangerous because believing this idea is new may lead us to abandon critical core components of our educational process that remain vital to the development of our economy and society. With limited resources, new ventures must, at least in part, replace old activities. We need to take great care to ensure that we replace only those older activities that are outdated and not those that are core to our future success as well.

Second, there is danger in the narrow focus of some of our educational and training activities. Too many of our education and training partnership efforts focus solely on providing job-specific skills—on providing quick turn-around to place the person in that "next job." But we educate our citizens for more than tomorrow's job. We educate the person for the many jobs of his or her future. And we also educate to sustain a special quality to our lives beyond work, both individually and collectively.

Third, there is danger that the new partnership between educational institutions and business could erode the historical partnership between our educational institutions and their students. Our new business/education partnerships reflect more than a subtle change in focus. While we have always known that business and industry benefit in a secondary way from our educational efforts, our traditional focus as educators has been to bond most closely with our students. Today, our focus more often provides the primary bond between the educational institution and a specific business, with the student/citizen expected to be the secondary beneficiary....

Larry Blake

Although education is not quite as foreign to the business world as Japanese, nevertheless, our management styles, measures of productivity, value systems, and even descriptive languages are different. We must now start merging our languages and our processes for mutual understanding. As an example, I am pleased to see that, at this conference we have such "noneducational" topics as economic development, technology transfer, small business development, international trade, and even human resource development. Although all of these terms are useful, I still prefer to communicate with my fellow educators through the redefinition of our three basic goals— namely, teaching, research, and public service.

In "teaching" we need to use the term *human resource development* and to recognize the changing needs of our environment, particularly in the economic sector with regard to preemployment education and, increasingly, continuing education.

In the "research" sector, we need to continue to work with basic research but increasingly develop applied research involving the research professor as entrepreneur, sponsored and cosponsored research, technology transfer, and industrial partnerships.

With regard to "public service," this definition needs to be extended to include such things as assisting small business and entrepreneurs through small business development centers, business incubators, etc.; providing demographic and other data services to elements of government; and serving economic development agencies and task forces by college personnel at the local, regional, state, and national levels....

In the teaching, or human resource development area, Oregon Tech has effectively utilized industrial advisory committees throughout its forty-year history, gaining advice regarding curricular currency, laboratory equipment, graduate preparation, and faculty qualifications. As a result of this close tie with business and industry, Oregon Tech boasts a 97-percent graduate placement rate for the past five years, a figure we believe to be the highest in the nation ,and well over a 90-percent placement rate for several decades....

With regard to research, although only a baccalaureate-granting institution at present, OIT solicits client-based proposals for senior projects from a wide range of business and industry, utilizing 30-50 percent of those proposals suggested. Because of an international expertise in geothermal energy, an internationally acclaimed Geo-Heat Research Center was established over a decade ago and continues to be in the forefront of this field. Currently, a superconductor research center is being proposed based on contracts already received by several faculty in this field. One faculty member has been awarded several Small Business Innovative Research grants, and another has just been awarded a grant entitled the Oregon Research and Technology Development Center from the state-based venture capital agency ....

Steven Altman

The underlying premise for our engagement in economic development activity is that the desired outcomes will occur through the development of human resources. The plan shows cognizance of and sensitivity to the abilities of businessmen and women to create positive economic gains and to fulfill satisfying goals. This is as important in South Texas as it is anywhere, but there is an urgency about responding to the ravaging effects of the oil and gas price crash and the continued instability in related markets, the similar (albeit not as abrupt) declines in agriculture and livestock economies, high unemployment, low per-capita income, limited educational access, and a rapidly changing social and demographic profile. In short, the region is isolated, poor, and suffering. If we can help people help themselves, then the long road to recovery will become evident.

The objectives of the U.S. Office of Economic Development are to: (a) foster entrepreneurship, (b) increase the efficiency of existing small businesses, (c) increase employment opportunities, (D) encourage the development of business research, (e) generate business-oriented data banks and libraries, (f) develop a conduit to technical transfer from the university to private business, and (g) promote capital investment in South Texas.

These objectives will be accomplished by providing information, business counseling, workshops, and expertise to existing and potential entrepreneurs in the region in order to improve their ability to compete in appropriate markets. The office will build bridges between the institution and the private sector to spur growth and provide jobs and thereby improve the quality of life in South Texas.

Some of the specific initiatives include: (a) training and assistance to increase the efficiency and effectiveness of existing small business firms, (b) reducing the failure rate of small businesses in the region, (c) attracting research dollars to South Texas, (d) advising potential entrepreneurs about the feasibility of new business ventures, (e) developing new industry in the region, (f) increasing the number of jobs in the region, and (g) fostering more involvement of businesses and the university in joint ventures....

Donald Gerth

One of the tasks of a regional university is to foster economic development. We can do this by:
• providing the people of the region with the preparation in the skills and expertise that participation in its particular economic environment requires....
• functioning as a repository and clearinghouse of knowledge and expertise....
• remembering that universities are places not only where knowledge is stored, inspected, and imparted to the young, but also where it is *created*....

Extension into new markets, especially if those markets are international, is not as easy as many American supporters of "free-trade" assume. There is much need for the knowledge and expertise that universities can provide.

In order to provide it, faculty in our school of business are organizing the "Pacific Rim Commercial Exchange Program" (PRCEP) with an international mission. Many institutions, government agencies, businesses, and even individuals are interested in Pacific Rim commercial relations; yet there are no "one-stop" sources of information and expertise.

PRCEP proposes to serve as just such a source. Its staff will run conferences, many in the form of international videoconferences, between representatives of different nations. The first proposed conference will take place this spring between Sacramento and other cities in California, and Brisbane, Sydney,

Melbourne, and Adelaide in Australia. The program will also sponsor an informational journal, *Pacific Connections,* which will contain a "New Developments" section highlighting new products or services of interest to Pacific Rim markets.

Many businesses in the Sacramento area have indicated that they lack essential information about foreign markets. They would be interested in "prequalifying" a market for their products before investing the needed effort. PRCEP plans to develop seminars and provide courses taught both by university faculty and other authorities to provide the information to do this. These courses will be developed with the assistance of chambers of commerce, law firms, and private corporations. The series of courses could ultimately develop into a credential program in international trade, providing knowledge on international finance, letters of credit, host country commercial law and practice, and language....

Ruth Leventhal

Governor Casey has proposed a broad-based economic development partnership between geographically and fiscally disparate public and private sectors of the state's economy, using a long-term strategy for economic revitalization. The basis of this plan was an extensive study originally sponsored by the Pennsylvania Business Roundtable, a group of thirty-eight Fortune 500 companies either headquartered or maintaining significant facilities in Pennsylvania. Using volunteer expert consultants from all over Pennsylvania, a plan was developed that proposed a path to a better future for the state in the next century.

The original plan from the Business Roundtable was adapted by the Casey administration, and each segment of higher education in the Commonwealth will play a role in the implementation of this plan. The Pennsylvania State University and other major research universities in the Commonwealth will work to ensure that competitiveness of the major industries in

Pennsylvania is maintained: first, by taking the lead in ensuring that Pennsylvania remains in a strong position in technology transfer through the establishment of statewide mechanisms for technology transfer programs; second, by hosting a summit on competitive positioning, bringing together the best minds to the university to plan the steps necessary to ensure a competitive economic position for the Commonwealth industries; third, by using resources to help support economic development, education, research, training, and statewide outreach for the maximum benefit of the Commonwealth; and finally, by continuing to explore the establishment of industry research centers at all appropriate university locations....

A number of broad-ranging services will be undertaken specifically by Penn State, including providing advisory services to government and promoting a business-sensitive environment within the university itself; supporting venture and equity investments; establishing state-of-the-art facilities in biotechnology and engineering; providing outreach assistance to business and industry through a variety of service centers; creating an environment that encourages faculty, staff, and students to engage in entrepreneurial activities; developing university land for a research park; and other activities such as business incubators and, of course, continuing research and technology transfer. All of these undertakings can be distributed throughout the 22-campus system of Penn State so that local impact, even in rural areas, will be great.

There are a number of bills in the Pennsylvania General Assembly now aimed at supporting other initiatives by higher education in rural economic development. Examples include centers for rural Pennsylvania that would provide rural adult education and adult literacy programs. Such centers would facilitate and coordinate basic and applied research and service opportunities for faculty, staff, and students in dealing with issues important to the welfare of rural Pennsylvanians through grant-supported programs that are administered by universities. The focus of such programs would include rural communities, economic development, local government, finance, administration, community services, natural resources and the environment, and educational outreach. Universities would be able to provide outreach and services to rural school districts and other rural groups, resulting in better utilization of the resources of the universities. Clearly, this would enhance efforts to improve the rates of literacy and increase participation in higher education by people in rural areas.

Other initiatives would support development of rural marketing, promotion and tourism, implementation of instructional and student development programs for rural students coming from economically disadvantaged backgrounds, establishment of rural, postsecondary services in financially depressed areas, and the Penn State expansion of its rural leadership training program. All these proposed legislative efforts would complement an existing model that has had an exciting, innovative, and effective impact on the Commonwealth over the last five years— the Ben Franklin Partnership Program, designed to bring together resources of business, educational institutions, and state government to fund joint projects for creating new jobs and retaining existing ones in Pennsylvania....

Patty Martillaro

The University of Colorado Small Business Assistance Center (SBAC) is a statewide program offering a full range of management and technical assistance, including procurement and export consulting. All our consultants are full-time employees, and we have six branch offices throughout Colorado. We are the economic development outreach arm of the University of Colorado.

Our initiative involves a forward-looking, cooperative arrangement with the NASA Industrial Application Center of the University of Southern California. Initial discussions began 4-1/2 years ago, when the director of the NASA Industrial Application Center, Radford King, and I began working on a way to combine the tremendous information and technology resources available through his NASA center with the grass-roots coverage afforded by our center in Colorado. To begin, we asked the question, "What are the needs of our businesses, including small business in rural areas, that we are not presently addressing and are desperately needed?" The answer was, "Instant access by the business to technology and up-to-date information at an affordable cost."

To make this cooperative arrangement successful, we thought the following criteria to be necessary:
• trained professionals who not only would be able to access information and technology but also would be able to understand business, economic development, and technical problems, thus providing the client direct access to the desired information or technology, the client playing the key role and being active in the process
• access to many commercial and public data bases and the ability to add to these data bases when we had a particular need
• training for the research staff at the University Small Business Assistance Center, to enable them to work with the client prior to accessing the professionals at NASA
• basic computer and software equipment
• access to a network of experts from NASA's federal and university laboratories in many disciplines who would be willing to consult with our center and clients when a solution could not be found through the search capabilities
• the ability to respond immediately to our businesses
• permission to put the work station outside our offices into economic development offices, incubators, community colleges, and in some cases, private companies throughout the state....

As you can well imagine, the uses for this system are limited only by one's imagination. In our first year we have used the system to:

• obtain expert opinions and new product information or application in the commercial production of dried flowers,
• locate the only manufacturer for a highly specialized product,
• search patent and trade-name records, resulting in thousands of dollars of savings to businesses,

• obtain market information for a new type of tour guide/conference-planning business that identified trends in the market, names and addresses of associations planning future conventions, and directories and resources to use for locating potential tour clients,

• analyze foreign markets for food products and recreational vehicles (size and share of market, projections, major competitors),

• construct mailing lists identifying contacts in other companies,

• identify top-ranking companies (by sales) in a certain field for an economic developer to approach relative to relocating a company to Colorado. The list provided information on each firm's financial status, sales, employment, major officers, new products, and biographies of some of the major officers....

Leon Boothe

There are many activities that a college or university can do that will cost little or nothing in terms of direct outlay of funding. Most institutions require faculty and major staff to fulfill a service to the community requirement. As such, many faculty can be available and welcome, within reason, consultation opportunities on any given subject. Carrying that same idea further, many classes from sociology to business can be of enormous help to a business by adopting it as a case study for a given time period. For example, I have a local business person who has expressed to me on a number of occasions his sincere thanks and appreciation to the university for saving his business. He was having some difficult problems and approached the university. A business class took on the project, made recommendations that he adopted and to which he credits the saving of his business, which is now flourishing. Very important to many businesses is the fact that student internships or co-ops can be an invaluable source for both business and the university as it relates to students gaining the applied practical experience that greatly broadens their educational base and, at the same time, aids businesses in terms of achieving some of their objectives. Other important ways in which colleges and universities can be of enormous help in terms of economic development is to have key individuals heavily involved in a chamber of commerce or, depending on the size of the urban area, a number of chambers. Realizing that the state government will have impact on any urban development, I would also suggest that a college or university maintain its ties with important offices in the state's capital so as to be involved as appropriate in foreign trade missions and other economic explorations that could have economic impact on a given urban setting.

With state resources becoming increasingly scarce and federal involvement through funding decreasing, many urban colleges and universities are increasingly turning to the privatization approach to campus needs and development. This is part of an effort to leverage nonstate sources to achieve the goals of the university. This can range from the erection of edifices from student housing to more sophisticated office complexes to having physical plant operations operated by private corporations. Such moves, of course, have economic implications and lead to further economic development. When venture capital can be found, there are clearly some opportunities that would provide payback. Most colleges and universities in this day and age have small business centers on their campuses. This helps to identify a large segment of the business community with the university, and the large segment of the business community with the university, and the interchange is quite rewarding. Some urban schools have developed development centers more broad based in terms of size of business as well as geographical area. In a more sophisticated move, some colleges and universities, such as my own, have developed research parks, which by their very nature enhance economic development in the area and, at the same time, provide continuing revenue for the university. In our particular case, there have been additional benefits to the institution in that the selected businesses coming into the area provide adjunct faculty for the institution as well as research opportunities for our regular faculty. Additionally, the businesses provide employment and research opportunities for large numbers of university students....

A new approach being taken by some urban universities is organizing research opportunities for faculty under the aegis of a foundation. Rather than having each faculty member market his or her own skills in the promotion of consultation skills, the foundation can become a clearinghouse for providing consultation opportunities with economic development overtones.

One approach seldom thought of in economic development is a public radio station on campus. It gives identity directly of the campus with the community. With such a community tie-in, focus is on needs and activities complementary to economic development interests....

Robert Carothers

Minnesota SURE (State University Research Enterprise) Access is a systemwide mechanism through which the human and physical resources of the Minnesota State University System will be applied to help meet the diverse needs of Minnesota businesses and communities. At the core of this mechanism is a comprehensive, up-to-date inventory of faculty, facilities, equipment, and organized resources that will be made widely accessible throughout Minnesota via an electronic catalog that will help network resources and advance cooperative research efforts between campuses and communities.

Through Minnesota SURE Access, faculty, staff, and students who might serve as consultants, research partners, or person power to develop and carry out research projects are being identified. In identifying these resources, care has been taken to look beyond exclusively scientific resources in order to fully include management, technical, marketing, and training expertise as well.

We believe that Minnesota SURE Access will provide a cost-effective means to provide, at small internal cost, a mechanism built on programs and resources already funded by the state. Its operation won't require new facilities or staff or the development of extensive (and expensive) new operating entities. The inventory that lies at the core of SURE Access will operate on our existing Data General computer network that ties all campuses together. Its operational structure will be similar to that of our academic computing network, with each campus designated as a center and with a single site providing a coordinating or clearinghouse function for the entire system. Ongoing development, operation, and refinement of SURE Access will be guided by an advisory council made up on one representative from each campus and a member of my staff.

Public access to the system by potential clients will be by telephone with a toll-free number to be put in place and widely marketed; the number will allow citizens anywhere in the state through a single telephone call to make contact with an individual campus or the central clearinghouse. Once a campus or clearinghouse connection has bee made, a contact person trained in "question negotiation," problem identification, and problem definition will define the problem, promise a response within five working days, and then search the data base. Once potentially appropriate sources of assistance are identified, contact will be made with gatekeepers on each appropriate campus who will then review the problem and identified resources, determine the current availability of those resources, and determine whether an institutional or individual response is appropriate. If individual faculty are identified, they will be contacted in order to determine their interest in pursuing the problem, and if they are agreeable, the client will be given the information needed to pursue project negotiation.

At present, faculty surveys are being completed on each campus, and we are gearing up to get the data entered in order to be prepared to become operational in April of this year. An internal reallocation of $150,000 is supporting the creation of Minnesota SURE Access, and initial efforts to raise external funding to support the system are being made. We have moved rapidly in order to turn our plans into reality in record time, and we can only estimate what the demand for assistance will be. Frankly, we don't know whether to be more concerned that users will demand more than we can provide or that telephones won't ring for weeks on end. We also know that there will be bugs to work out and modifications to make. As a result, we are preparing to phase in our marketing as we grow more confident that the system is operating effectively and that we are providing a real service to the people of Minnesota. But while we are taking care not to build a momentum we can't sustain, we are, nevertheless, moving ahead aggressively to put in place a system we believe will provide assistance to individuals and businesses throughout the state and, as a result, help advance the state's economic vitality. When we broadly proclaim that the collective resources of the Minnesota State University System are "as close as your telephone" anywhere in Minnesota, we have every confidence that we will be able to satisfy those who ask us to live up to our word.

John Woodward

Although not new to you, the key to what works in economic development comes down to *local leadership*.

Several years ago, nearly everyone was coming to EDA for incubator buildings. Requests were so widespread that we concluded that many requesters were attending the same conferences. Our experience shows that incubators worked or failed directly in proportion to local leadership and commitment to render effective backup services to start-up businesses.

You cannot duplicate someone else's idea in economic development with any guarantee of success. At your campuses, you need to inventory your strengths, inventory economic needs of your area, and make the best possible management or bridges to deliver the strengths of your institution to those in need....

It is critical that your institution's leadership be committed to whatever program or approach is selected. Without the support of those with policy-making responsibilities, your efforts are likely to have minimal impact.

It is also critical that the institution develop its role in cooperation with other area organizations and individuals with economic development responsibilities. This strategy should help prevent duplication of effort and ensure coordination of related activities.

As exemplified by some of the success stories presented at this conference, colleges and universities are perfectly capable of embarking on economic development activities without federal support. Given dwindling federal resources and the deplorable budget deficit, looking to the feds for funding is clearly not the way to ensure a successful program.

Nonetheless, I should mention that EDA administers a small university center program designed to provide seed funds to help institutions of higher education initiate activities designed to address local, regional, or statewide economic development problems. Our policy is to provide start-up funding of $100,000 annually for five years and lesser amounts for two additional years. During the funding period, the institution receiving support is expected to obtain increasing amounts of support from other sources.

But don't come to us for funding if you don't have your act together with respect to support from your institution's leadership, some financing from other sources, and coordination with other organizations and individuals involved in economic development in the area you intend to serve....